Mid-Victorian Masterpiece

*The story of an institution
unable to put its own
house in order*

BARNETT COCKS

MID-VICTORIAN MASTERPIECE

The story of an institution
unable to put its own house in order

HUTCHINSON OF LONDON

Hutchinson & Co (Publishers) Ltd
3 Fitzroy Square, London W1

London Melbourne Sydney Auckland
Wellington Johannesburg and agencies
throughout the world

First published 1977
© Barnett Cocks 1977

Set in Monotype Fournier

Printed in Great Britain by The Anchor Press Ltd
and bound by Wm Brendon & Son Ltd
both of Tiptree Essex

ISBN 0 09 128260 8

To Iris

CONTENTS

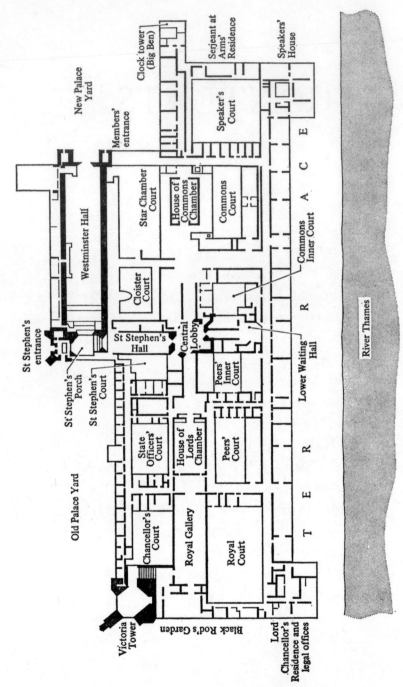

The new Houses of Parliament (completed 1870) showing Barry's eleven courtyards and principal floor plan

ILLUSTRATIONS

Between pages 80 and 81

Portrait of Sir Charles Barry (by permission of Ashmolean Museum, Oxford)

Augustus Welby Pugin (by permission of National Portrait Gallery)

The old Houses of Parliament before the great fire of 1834 (by courtesy of House of Lords Record Office)

Westminster Hall (by permission of *Illustrated London News*)

Houses of Parliament – the landward side (by permission of Fox Photos)

Edward M. Barry (by courtesy of House of Lords Record Office)

The Fine Arts Commission (National Portrait Gallery)

The Crypt Chapel (*Illustrated London News*)

The new Houses of Parliament, 1835 (Public Record Office)

House of Commons Chamber, 1852 (*Illustrated London News*)

St Stephen's Hall (Fox Photos)

Members on the Terrace (*Illustrated London News*)

The new Houses of Parliament from the river (Fox Photos)

Between pages 144 and 145

Star Chamber Court (*Illustrated London News*)

Star Chamber Court after infilling (Fox Photos)

A view of the carriageway (by permission of Harry Kerr)

Parliament and Bridge Street (Fox Photos)

Commons Chamber after German air raid, 1941 (by permission of Keystone Press)

The Clock Tower against a foreground of fire, 1974 (by permission of Associated Press)

ACKNOWLEDGEMENTS

No author can claim all the credit for a book which appears under his name. Without the encouragement of Mr David Higham, my literary agent, who introduced me to Mr Charles Clark of Hutchinson, I could not have started. Without the qualities of the publishers' gifted staff – Mr Julian Watson's judgement, Miss Frankie Cormac's patience and Mr Christopher Chippindale's perception – I might never have finished.

Words failed me when it came to describing recent additions to the architectural masterpiece of the nineteenth century; but Mr Harry Kerr provided a splendid commentary in his photographs.

I despaired of finding a portrait of Edward Middleton Barry, but Mr Maurice Bond, whose work I also describe in the final chapter, was kind enough to provide the photograph by J. E. Mayall in addition to the etching by J. Bryant.

Mr Mike Roffey gave me access to the comprehensive collection in The Times Photo Library. The Illustrated London News and Sketch Ltd, through their Archives Manager, Mr H. E. Bray, allowed me to reproduce drawings.

Other organizations were equally ready to assist me with copies of pictures or photos from their collections.

Books which proved most valuable in my researches were:

The History of the King's Works Vol. VI by J. Mordaunt Crook and M. H. Port, HMSO, 1973.

The Gothic Revival by Kenneth Clark, John Murray, 1962.

Pugin by Phoebe Stanton, Thames & Hudson, 1971.

Pictorial History of English Architecture by John Betjeman, John Murray, 1972.

Parliament House by Maurice Hastings, Architectural Press, 1950.

CHAPTER ONE

PARLIAMENT IN FLAMES

1834

Darkness had already fallen on a fine October night in 1834 when the sky over Westminster suddenly began to glow, first orange and then red, as in a late sunset. Flames shot up above the shabby congeries of walls and towers which comprised the old Palace of Westminster, where the Houses of Parliament had been meeting for centuries past. Before the night was over, it seemed that it would be a long time before either House would be able to meet there again. Apart from Westminster Hall, the whole Palace had caught alight.

Only two years before, a new Clerk of Works, Richard Whibley, had been given responsibility for the fabric of the Houses of Parliament by virtue of his appointment to the pretentious post of 'Labourer in Trust'. Divided responsibility existed in everything concerning the King's palace and the people's parliamentary buildings, and when the parliament met at Westminster within a royal palace a clash of jurisdictions was inevitable, and conflicts between the authorities were as frequent then as they are today.

The new Clerk of Works sought to make his mark and to display his crusading efficiency by clearing some of the superfluous rubbish which had accumulated around Westminster Hall, which was then as now the largest individual structure within the precincts of the Palace. The setting up by the House of Commons of a Select Committee in 1833, the year before the fire, to look into the possibility of making the premises more commodious and 'less unwholesome' for Members was also a spur to action by the officials of the House.

The Exchequer Office which adjoined Westminster Hall had many years earlier ceased to use the old accounting system of tallies, which were sticks notched to show the different amounts levied on each taxpayer. It was a primitive method of reckoning by which the sticks were split vertically, one half being held by the Exchequer and the other by the taxpayer. Whibley aimed to destroy a great number of these wooden tallies and conceived what appeared to be both an economical and discreet plan for disposing of these obsolete tokens. The Exchequer Office probably thought they should be disposed of with caution and dignity and not merely shovelled into the river as jetsam, which was then the normal means of rubbish disposal. Whibley therefore arranged that they should be burned in the furnaces which heated the flues under the floor of the House of Lords. After some hours the tallies were burning merrily, generating such an intense amount of flame and smoke that the flues became over-heated. Two workmen were busy piling the tally sticks into the furnaces. They had to get rid of two cart-loads, and had been told to dampen the sticks with water to prevent them burning too fast. Anyone concerned in the employment of men would know how much attention would be paid to an instruction of that kind. The workmen were piling on the wood all day to create, to their delight, an astonishing blaze.

At ten o'clock that morning, Mrs Wright, the housekeeper, went into the empty House of Lords and noticed smoke and a smell of burning wood. She did not consult higher authority; the hereditary keeper of the Palace was the Lord Great Chamberlain, and never in living memory had such an exalted official been seen on the premises except when a visit of the Sovereign was impending. At half past three that afternoon, Mrs Wright did find the courage and indignation to complain. Not of course to the Clerk of Works, who would have given short shrift to such a subordinate person, and a woman at that, but she expressed her concern to one of the two workmen. She said the House was in a complete smother and the throne could scarcely be seen; but the workman retorted that he couldn't help his orders, he'd been told to burn the tallies and he'd finish the job in about an hour.

At four o'clock, two visitors asked to see the interior of the House of Lords. Through their shoes they felt the heat of the stone floor and because of the smoke they could not even see the magnificent tapestries on the walls. Where was the Speaker of the Lords, where was the Clerk of the Parliaments, where was Black Rod, where was the Serjeant-at-Arms, where were all those with responsibility for the custody of a Palace which housed the records of a thousand years of history? The answer is the same as it was a century later in 1941 when, after due notice, German incendiaries were dropped on the building – the highest officers were away in the country; it is certain that on the October evening of 1834 they were content to leave the responsibility to Mrs Wright. She locked the door of the House at five o'clock without reporting her fears to any of her superiors. There was no nightwatchman but there was a doorkeeper somewhere around. It was at six o'clock that evening that Mrs Mullencamp, his wife, noticed a light flickering under the door of the House of Lords and gave the alarm. A few minutes later the building burst into flames.

It was a major outbreak of fire which the primitive fire-engines of those days did their best to extinguish but could not contain. A conflagration began to envelop both Houses; it soon spread to the Commons Library, lobbies and offices, all of which were burnt out by midnight.

Joseph Hume, the radical MP, had tabled a motion for better accommodation for Members. 'Mr Hume's motion for a new House is carried without a division,' remarked a cynical onlooker.

It was an age when large-scale excitements were fewer than today. 'The progress of the fire exhibited a *tableau vivant* of not inferior interest,' said a contemporary observer. 'The wind blew briskly from the south-west, but became more southerly as the night advanced; the moon was near the full and shone with radiance; but occasionally vast masses of cumulus clouds floated high and bright across the skies and, as the fitful glare of the flames increased, were illuminated in a remarkably impressive manner, which gave great interest to the busy scene that was passing below. . . . An immense multitude of spectators assembled at Westminster to witness the ravages of the fire, the lurid glare of which was distinctly visible for many miles around the metropolis. Even the river Thames, in the vicinity of the spot, was covered with boats and barges full of persons whom curiosity had attracted to the scene; and the reflections of the wavering flames upon the water, on the neighbouring shores and on the many thousands thus congregated, composed a spectacle most strikingly picturesque and impressive. . . .'

By this time the working parties of firemen and soldiers were having to cope not only with the blaze but with the constantly growing numbers of onlookers. Now some great men began to make their appearance. There was the Dean of Westminster, who was anxious for the safety of the Abbey, and, finally, the Prime Minister himself, Lord Melbourne, who personally directed attempts to save Westminster Hall from being engulfed. Fire engines were brought inside the Hall in order to play water on the irreplaceable hammer-beam roof which had been added to William Rufus's original building when Geoffrey Chaucer was the Clerk of Works. St Stephen's Chapel, where the Commons had sat since 1547, however, and many of the other buildings which comprised the Palace were burnt out, together with innumerable manuscripts, tapestries and paintings.

It was not till nearly three o'clock in the morning that the fire was at last brought under control, and the shock of the disaster was felt throughout England. Early news had already been sent out to the cities and countryside by the fastest way then known. It was scrawled at the foot of the passenger lists carried by the horse-drawn coaches as they left London. Wherever the coaches stopped to change horses, the news was read. The guard of the night mail coach carried the first announcement to Birmingham, some hundred and ten miles away, by breakfast time the next morning. At first it was thought to be a joke. But the newspapers confirmed the notices on the coaches, 'At this moment both Houses of Parliament are in flames.' As a London-bound coach passed through Oxford, the students of Christ Church College shouted to the guard, 'You will not be in time to see the Lord Chancellor's wig on fire.'

Those whose duty required them to live in the Palace lost many personal possessions. Rare manuscripts, desks, chairs and tapestries were rescued and unceremoniously dumped outside, only to receive a ruinous soaking from the firemen's hoses.

Charles Manners-Sutton, the confessedly Tory Speaker, was unlucky in having suffered the heaviest losses in the fire. His fine furniture, much of which had been stored in the lumber rooms of the House of Commons, was insured with the Sun Insurance Company for several thousand pounds, together with his personal library of valuable books. In the summer of 1832, the Speaker had informed the House that he intended to retire and because he was about to move out he allowed his policy to lapse. Early in the following year, the newly elected Whig government persuaded him to stay on because they needed his experience. He then overlooked the need to restore his insurance cover and, in consequence, he estimated he had suffered a loss of £9000 worth of goods for which he held the government responsible, since the carelessness of their staff led to the disaster.

Lesser officials followed the august example of the Speaker in putting in claims. The deputy housekeeper, Bellamy, whose father's pies were allegedly fancied by the dying Pitt, had wisely maintained an insurance policy on his personal effects for £1500 on which British Life Insurance obligingly paid out £1425 although the policy itself had been burned in the fire. Bellamy, however, still asked to be reimbursed with another £400.

One of the clerks remembered such items as a cornelian ring and manuscripts left in a desk, which he assessed as together worth £20. The smallest claim was made by William Bevan, a messenger, who sought to be compensated for a dress hat at 10s. 6d., a pair of court shoes at 10s. 0d. and a pair of buckles at 12s. 0d.

Three years later, all the losses were still being disputed in an increasingly angry series of letters from Manners-Sutton, now pensioned off as Viscount Canterbury, to the Office of Works, to the Chancellor of the Exchequer and, finally, to Melbourne himself as Prime Minister. The obdurate refusal of the government to pay for any of the Speaker's losses in the fire foreshadowed a resolute meanness towards any other claims upon the public purse, from which the architect for the rebuilding was destined to become the chief victim.

The fire of 1834 could not have come as an unlooked-for event, but it was nevertheless dramatic in its immediate impact. For generations the Members of the House of Commons had come reluctantly to Westminster from the far pleasanter settings of the shires or towns in which they all lived in spacious comfort or even luxury. There were no socialists and little cognizance of differences in wealth, since all elected representatives were more or less well endowed with great estates or possessed of great industrial and commercial resources. Members were united in distaste for the way in which they were housed for their deliberations within the Royal Palace of Westminster.

In 1547, during the minority rule of Edward VI, the Protector Somerset had handed over St Stephen's Chapel as a debating chamber for the Commons. It was in line with the attitudes of post-Reformation England that a formerly consecrated chapel, once its considerable wealth had been confiscated, should be debased for the uses of an upstart assembly of no great repute. What was good enough in 1547 was little changed over the years. Towards the end of the eighteenth century a Lutheran pastor, Moritz, wrote: 'I now for the first time saw the whole of the British nation assembled in its representatives in a rather mean-looking building that not a little resembles a chapel. . . . The Members have nothing particular in their dress. . . . It is not at all uncommon to see a Member lying stretched out on one of the benches while others are debating. Some crack nuts, others eat oranges or whatever else is in season.'

It was a fair picture and immediately recognizable even today, except that in recent times eating in the debating chamber – as distinct from sipping a beverage for the throat's sake – has been deprecated by the Speaker.

The chapel only measured twenty paces by ten, and in 1833, only a year before the fire, William Cobbett vainly asked, 'Why are we squeezed into so small a space that it is absolutely impossible that there should be calm and regular discussion. . . . Why do we live in this hubbub? . . . Why are 658 of us crammed into a space which allows to each of us no more than a foot and a half square?'

Outside St Stephen's, the offices and committee rooms were also inadequate, while the ugly and squalid confusion which surrounded the great Hall of Westminster formed a continuing invitation to disaster from fire.

The maintenance of the Palace of Westminster fell within the jurisdiction of a minor Department of State – the Office of Works – whose authority derived from the Lord Chamberlain's office. Large-scale alterations were however paid for by specific parliamentary grants. At the end of the eighteenth century, there was ground for some not untypical confusion. The Clerk of the Works, Sir John Soane, delegated minor undertakings to his resident Labourer in Trust, whose charge covered both Houses of Parliament and Westminster Hall. Larger works involved the royal if nominal occupier of the Palace – King George III, whose architect, James Wyatt, held views almost inevitably opposed to those of Sir John Soane. The control of the whole group of buildings was vested in the Lord Great Chamberlain, a hereditary officer of state who intermittently had to remind lesser mortals that he was not for one moment to be confused with the Lord Chamberlain.

A separate authority, the Commissioners for Westminster Improvements, also had a role to play. Thus while repairs at the Court of the Exchequer adjoining Westminster Hall were dealt with by the Court's own officers, the two coffee houses beneath the Exchequer fell to the Surveyor to the Commissioners for Westminster Improvements, who in another capacity was Labourer in Trust. Lest it be thought that there was some reasonable co-ordination of responsibility here, it must be explained that the coffee house at the north end of Westminster Hall, a few paces from the other two coffee houses, was under the jurisdiction of the Westminster Bridge Commissioners.

In 1814–15 reforms placed the Palace of Westminster in the care of an 'Attached Architect' (Sir John Soane) with control over a Clerk of the Works and a Labourer in Trust. In 1832, a further reform swept away both the Attached Architect and the Clerk of the Works, and the fabric of the Houses of Parliament became the responsibility of the Labourer in Trust, himself newly designated as

Clerk of the Works. Officialdom was ill prepared for an emergency.

A vivid picture of the whole area was contained in a contemporary report for the House of Commons signed by no less than fourteen architects, including Robert Adam and James Wyatt. 'On the west side of St Stephen's Court, against the East Wall of Westminster Hall are the Coach Houses and Stables of the Auditor of the Exchequer, having hay lofts and servants' lodging rooms over them, which adjoin and come close under the windows of the office and cash room of one of the Tellers of the Exchequer. . . . The Court of Exchequer and Exchequer Chamber, contiguous to and connected with Westminster Hall are very old, but not in a state of actual ruin.'

But the rooms below, with ceilings and walls lined with deal, were reported as being insecure from fire and the coffee houses were particularly dangerous as they had several chimneys and coppers and some of the wooden roofs were 'covered with Sail Cloth pitched'.

Writing in 1800, John Carter demanded 'Away with these usurping excrescences of sheds, hovels, taverns and alehouses that blot out and disfigure the walls of old English splendour. . . .' A limited clearing up was indeed undertaken.

The catastrophe was not unexpected by those who had studied the structure of the Palace. Sir John Soane wrote six years earlier in his *Designs for Public Buildings*: 'The exterior of these old buildings as well as the interior is constructed chiefly of timber covered with plaster. In such an extensive assemblage of combustible materials, what would become of the Painted Chamber, the House of Commons and Westminster Hall? The want of security from fire calls loudly for revision and speedy amendment.'

The authorities, in accordance with the usual scepticism when laymen are faced with alarums sounded by experts, did nothing before the event to prevent its taking place; but they went into action as soon as it was over. First it was necessary to attribute the blame; the public who had witnessed the disaster had cheered and clapped as the roofs fell in, and their enjoyment awoke suspicions that there might be a conspiracy afoot. Plots, like Parliament, were always closely associated with political events, and a London tradesman came forward to swear that on the night of the fire he was in Dudley,

119 miles away, and was told the news three hours after the fire broke out. This would have been impossible, in days before the telegraph, unless there was a deliberate and pre-arranged plan to set fire to Parliament. The government took the story seriously enough to institute an investigation by a committee of the Privy Council. A succession of witnesses were summoned from the coaching inns of old England to give their bibulous testimony to the Lords of the Privy Council on how quickly the news had reached them, and when the first news had been heard in each town. After a fortnight of intensive inquiry, the Privy Council were satisfied that no news had travelled faster than the coach horses and that consequently no plot had caused Parliament's destruction by fire.

Meanwhile the King's Ministers had to make some arrangements, albeit of a makeshift and temporary character, to house both the Lords and the Commons when they returned to their respective sittings at Westminster after the long summer recess. Lord Melbourne as Prime Minister played for safety by asking an experienced government architect, Sir Robert Smirke, to prepare a plan both for temporary accommodation and for rebuilding the Houses of Parliament on 'a moderate and suitable scale of magnitude'. Smirke reported within a few days that in spite of the devastating fire, the walls of the House of Lords and those of the Painted Chamber were still standing and roofs could be built over them. The Painted Chamber was fitted up with a throne and three rows of seats on each side for the peers; while the burned-out House of Lords was redesigned for the Commons as their assembly hall. These temporary Houses were ready for use by 17 February 1835, a feat of remarkable rapidity, achieved by working through the night.

CHAPTER TWO

A WINNING DESIGN

1836

The horses of the coach from Brighton pulled their weary load over the long range of hills south of London and began the long descent into the river valley of the Thames, through the Southwark stews, which were already unsavoury in Shakespeare's day, and on towards Westminster. The passengers on the coach were excitedly speculating on the cause of the great fire which they saw blazing over Parliament. Among them was Charles Barry, a reasonably prosperous architect, returning from a business trip to the growing coastal town.

He was soon hurrying to the scene to join the great crowd of spectators; although he would not for a moment have rejoiced over such wanton damage, he remained till dawn to assess not only the loss but the extent of the rebuilding which would be required. Next day he called on his young and brilliant colleague, twenty-two-year-old Augustus Welby Pugin, to discuss the prospects for the future. Neither could have foreseen that more than a century later historians would be debating the respective contributions of each to the development of English architecture.

Yet Barry was already forming the intention of playing a part, indeed the leading part, in replacing what the fire had, from his viewpoint, so helpfully cleared away. The blazing sky above Parliament was the sign he had long been waiting for. He saw himself crowning his career with a great new building in place of the confused huddle of roofs and turrets of the old Palace of Westminster, which were now falling before the irresistible onslaught of fire. Barry immediately realized that 'the erection of a new building was inevitable on a scale, and with an opportunity for the exercise of architectural genius, hitherto unexampled in England'. It was two years after the passing of the Great Reform Bill of 1832, and it was appropriate that the newly elected Members should have a building worthy of their expectations.

Barry was by any modern standard a self-educated man, a fact which it is important to recall in assessing the intellectual resources with which he had to meet the many crises of his remarkable career. He was born on 23 May 1795 in a modest house in Bridge Street, Westminster, opposite the Houses of Parliament. His father was a stationer who supplied materials to the government stationery office. Unfortunately, the stationer's wife died when Barry, her fourth son, was aged three. His father married again a few years later but himself died when Barry was only ten. The family was left in the care of Sarah, his step-mother, a good woman who brought up the children with care and affection. Barry and his brothers went to three schools, at one of which 'the master paid little attention, being very dissolute and absenting himself for weeks together'. He left the third and last school at fifteen with only a superficial knowledge of English, fair proficiency in arithmetic and remarkably good handwriting.

After this deficient schooling, Barry became articled to a small firm of architects and surveyors, Messrs Middleton & Bailey of Paradise Row, Lambeth. Here he made his mark; his first drawing was accepted for the architectural section of the Royal Academy's annual exhibition in 1812, when he was only seventeen. It depicted the interior of Westminster Hall – a subject to which he was to return later in his career.

Barry grew up in a London which today is sometimes portrayed as picturesque. The life of the city was still based on the countryside which supported it so closely; the cesspools of filth familiar to countrymen raised no surprise in the streets of London. There was fresh water of a kind, taken direct in pails from pumps at street corners or from the river, but in most cases it was contaminated with sewage and a ready source of cholera which in a bad year accounted for thousands of deaths.

The streets were crowded not only with the ragged and diseased populace of a city already reaching two million, but also with herds of cattle, their rumps and hooves thick with excrement, squealing pigs, shabby long-coated sheep, fowls already glaze-eyed and half dead in closed baskets piled up on handcarts, innumerable caged blackbirds, thrushes and other fauna from the countryside all destined for sale in the city markets. Slaughtering of the animals before or after sale was done in more than 150 uncontrolled slaughterhouses, in sheds, backyards or even cellars, fragments of hooves or skulls being thrown into the roadway for the scavenging dogs and rats.

There were no drains except for the occasional open gutter blocked with urine, offal and bloody remnants of all kinds.

Against that background, the young Barry was dreaming of towers, gardens and palaces with an inner confidence that he could and would create them himself. In 1817 he decided to use his share of the small amount of money left by his father to embark on an ambitious grand tour of Europe and the Near East, in order to continue his study of architecture. Society was awakening from the torpor and isolation forced on England by years of European wars and Barry decided that travel would make up for the gaps in his knowledge and justify spending most or all of his small legacy. Beyond that, he had no means, but that did not prevent him from becoming engaged to another stationer's daughter, Sarah Rowsell, whom he had known for the past year. With that decision made, Barry, now aged twenty-one, confidently left England in June 1817 travelling alone; he did not return until August 1820. Of those three years he said later that one day abroad was 'worth a year at home'. So much has since been attributed to the help he got from Augustus Welby Pugin that his own early development is vital for a correct appreciation of his later work. He was a true artist and only later in his life did circumstances force him to adapt himself to a mould created by his employers.

Barry had a buoyant readiness to enjoy everything he came across, although he was cautious enough to go armed. He travelled by sailing ship to Rouen and then by horse-drawn coach to Paris. The Louvre occupied him for days but he dismissed modern artists such as David as showy and unnatural.

His study of buildings was always comprehensive and his criticisms, even from the first, were audaciously defiant of current fashion and authority. A small Corinthian church in Rouen got more attention than the great cathedral. Cemeteries always attracted his attention, but he disliked over-embellishment and preferred the sombre solemnity of a Turkish burial ground. In his diary he describes an encounter with soldiery who objected to his sketching in a small Italian town. They entered his bedroom and insisted on his leaving immediately, but Barry faced them out with a drawn pistol and they had to content themselves with posting a sentry outside his door. In Naples, he records his impression of the Toledo as 'the finest street, except the High Street of Oxford, I ever saw'.

From Italy he moved on to Greece, crossing from Bari in the only vessel available, a small felucca. Again he spent weeks of careful study, sketching and criticizing the masterpieces of Greek art before travelling onwards by sea and land to Constantinople, a journey which he described as 'one continued delight' in which natural beauty and cloudless skies pleased him as much as architectural marvels.

In 1818, after a month's stay in Turkey, he was offered a salary of £200 a year to travel further east with a Mr David Baillie, on condition that the latter might keep the originals of any sketches Barry might make. The offer meant a chance to see Egypt and Syria, and was too tempting to refuse. So far as he knew, Egypt had never before been explored by an English architect and its temples and monuments astonished him by their magnificence. The great temple at Dendera impressed him deeply, not only because of its immense size but because the ornaments and hieroglyphics covering its pillars and porticos opened for him an entirely new field of architecture. The impression made on him by the mixture of general grandeur of outline and dimension with profuse richness of detail was never effaced. Temple after temple inspired him; some 500 sketches for Mr Baillie and his own diary described what was then an almost unknown treasure house of ruins, equal in interest for him to the Parthenon in Greece.

Barry returned from his journey to the Near East by way of the Lebanon and Syria, taking in Baalbek and Damascus. Revisiting Italy, he gave close attention to Italian palaces. At first sight these travels seem a long way from Barry's subsequent work at Westminster. In fact, what he saw and noted with admiration became the foundation of many of his designs in the new Palace of Westminster. Again, he appreciated the richness and elaboration of the exterior of Milan's cathedral but not without criticism of its proportion: 'The pinnacles rise too suddenly out of the solid mass to an enormous height: the lantern spire is far too slender for the substructure.' Of the general design, he writes: 'much of its laboured enrichment is misapplied; there is a want of harmony and continuity in its parts and the sensation is created of wonder at the treasures lavished upon it, rather than of genuine admiration'.

To plan irregularity because it was picturesque he thought unworthy of the dignity of art. Every feature, especially every ornamental feature, ought in his mind to be rigidly subordinated to the preservation of the main outline and the main principle of the design, even at the cost of boldness and variety. Next, the exterior of a building should always indicate the internal design. Showy façades which in Italy often screened a mean building seemed to him impostures, worthy of contempt. He loved spaciousness. When he entered a building, he measured at a glance its utmost capacity, and all that stood in the way, such as piers and columns, he regarded as obstructions which he longed to clear away. In all great oblong halls the door should be at one end so that the whole interior could be seen at first entrance. It was a principle which he never willingly gave up. Finally, he believed that the mingling of grandeur with pettiness, of rich decoration with bare and unadorned features was an offence against harmony, and that mastery of an art was shown in the study and adaptation of every detail, almost as much as in the conception of a general design.

His last months abroad were marked by intense enjoyment in his self-appointed tasks. At Vicenza, for example, he found many of Palladio's villas were scattered in out-of-the-way places in the neighbourhood. Hiring a gig, he made his way over bad roads to track down, with minimal local information, everything he wanted to see. At one building there was some foliage which he wanted to sketch by artificial light; he got ladders and torches and proceeded with his work till he was stopped by the police.

After these three arduous and exciting years, Barry left Europe well acquainted with Greek, Egyptian and Italian architecture, and with a new appreciation of the reviving Gothic. At the same time he was not bound by the traditions of any single school, and felt confident enough to think and work for himself. The hopes with which he had gone abroad had been fully realized; he felt he had now educated himself in his chosen profession as an architect and returned to England ready to face any challenge.

In August 1820 Barry settled in London to begin his professional life. He took a small house in Ely Place, Holborn, which was unpretentious, cheap and central. His own friends and those of his future wife's middle-class family had the will but not the means to help him. In Rome he had received favourable notice from influential English travellers such as the Marquess of Lansdowne, but no patronage. The leading architects of the day were Nash, Smirke, Wyatt and Sir John Soane. He knew nothing of the first three and had encountered Soane only once in connection with some Islington church building. Grecian columns and porticos were still the fashion, and Barry with his new imaginative ideas from Europe and the Near East began the harassing and thankless work of public competition in which his designs were frequently rejected.

Among his earlier fruitless plans were those for Newington church, Kensington church, the Leeds Exchange, Streatham church, the Law Society, a new concert room in Manchester, alterations to Drummond castle, Bognor improvements, the Pitt Press in Cambridge, Highgate church, Charing Cross hospital, Birmingham town hall, Westminster hospital, a design for the National Gallery, a City club and a Manchester club. Occasionally in these years he felt despondent enough to contemplate emigrating to America. He had little money left after his overseas travels and his marriage had to be further deferred. His Egyptian sketches, unique at that time, might have brought him financial rewards but their projected publication was never realized, possibly because a written text to accompany the drawings was beyond his capacity.

Still he worked on. The Gothic revival was now asserting its claims, especially for ecclesiastical architecture. In dealing with church clients, however, he found that extensive requirements were usually backed by very limited resources. He spoke ruefully of a clergyman who was in negotiation with him as 'an Evangelical preacher with a great idea of building churches for nothing'. His first works of any consequence were two churches for the Church Commissioners, one at Prestwich and one at Campfield, Manchester. His letters show the exultation with which he hailed this first success. The complacency with which he regarded his first church designs changed in later years when these two churches became a continual subject of laughter for his friend Pugin and himself, so deficient were they in their lack of Gothic detail.

His success in getting two important contracts for the churches enabled him to marry on 7 December 1822.

One of Barry's most valuable ideas was that of 'architectural gardening'. He loved nature, and his houses, such as that for Mr Attree, a Brighton solicitor, were set whenever possible in terraced gardens such as Barry had seen in Italy.

In 1828 he entered a competition for building the Travellers Club in Pall Mall in which he adopted the Italian style. The lines of the Club were of splendid proportion and finish, and the work was original in that nothing in England preceded it, though it had many later imitations. In 1833–6 he designed King Edward's School, Birmingham, in Tudor Gothic, and in 1837 he designed Highclere Castle, Hampshire, in an Anglo-Italian style. A few years earlier he had built the City Art Gallery, Manchester, in the Greek tradition.

Barry's versatility enabled him to win the award for the most important building of the century – the new Houses of Parliament. For it was parliamentarians not architects who were to decide both what it should look like and how much it should cost. The government thought it proper to allow a public competition for the design of the new Houses of Parliament, but the designs had to follow a Gothic or Elizabethan style. Most of the grand mansions of the eighteenth century had been built in a severe but beautiful classical tradition, with tall oblong windows admitting a maximum amount of light and, if necessary, air. Arched window-frames and mullioned windows with a plenitude of turrets and pinnacles had formed the settings for Sir Walter Scott's novels and were in the forefront of popular taste, suggesting medieval English ancestry, as distinct from Romanesque lineage. It became the fashion to imitate the Middle Ages, and with the need to harmonize the new Parliament with Westminster Abbey and Westminster Hall, Barry felt that Gothic answered the needs of Members and the wishes of the public in general.

The time allowed for the competition was only six months, rather too short to prepare adequately the many drawings required by plans for a great Gothic edifice. Barry worked feverishly through many virtually sleepless nights. The first designs were striking both in their boldness and beauty of detail. Barry set out the lines with assured draughtsmanship and clarity, and Pugin enriched them with decoration. Out of 97 complete designs submitted, Barry's was number 64. He had neither influence nor support, and when he was pronounced the winner it was very clearly on grounds of merit alone.

The Commissioners who recommended his design envisaged an expenditure of £800000 over six years, and already, before any work was put in hand, they were exercised by considerations of cost, noting that the internal courtyards in Barry's plan would not need any enrichment of detail as they would not be visible to the general public but only to the occupants of the Palace.

Charles Barry's achievement in winning the competition against so many rivals delighted him; bitterness was to come later. Indeed he was never again exempt from disappointment, injustice and misrepresentation. His earlier years had been zestful and creative, in spite of handicaps which would have daunted a less resilient optimist than himself, but from now on he would be working under almost continuous denunciation.

The Report of the Royal Commissioners was approved by a Select Committee in each House and the first vote of money was passed by the Commons, not without some opposition, in July 1837. Meanwhile unsuccessful competitors began to attack the Barry plan in what soon became a sustained campaign of denigration.

The choice of Gothic instead of Greek or Roman styles was denounced, but a merit of Barry's work was that he was not committed to one particular school. He had to find a design with some relationship to the conglomeration of buildings which made up the old Palace of Westminster, and of which Westminster Hall at least was to remain, with the twin towers of the Abbey in the background.

When the vicious but still legitimate criticism of Barry's design did not seem likely to overthrow the decision of the Royal Commission in his favour, a petition on behalf of his disappointed rivals was presented to Parliament by Joseph Hume, the most persistent of all the critics in the Commons. The petition alleged that the rules for the competition had been ignored and expense had not been taken into account by the Commission.

In a debate which followed the presentation of the petition, Hume sounded an alarm at the prospect of large expenditure. This emphasis on cost was first to embarrass and later to harass Barry at every stage of the work. The House of Commons characteristically wanted the best, but were unwilling to pay for much more than the worst – champagne on beer money. Inevitably, this approach got them less than the best that their architect was capable of giving, yet rather more than their parsimony deserved. The immediate object of the petition was a further investigation of the whole problem, overturning the decision in favour of Barry's plan. This was resisted by Sir Robert Peel, the former Prime Minister, who pointed out that the whole principle of public competition would be destroyed if an award was subsequently rejected. Prophetically, Peel expressed sympathy for the successful competitor as a man already 'hunted and pursued' and whose victory would prove fatal for him. It became clear that the opposition was almost entirely inspired by unsuccessful competitors, and their aims were temporarily defeated. Misrepresentation of the architect's work and criticism of all he did was to continue, however.

Criticism of Barry was made in ignorance of his own inclinations and without appreciating the restrictions imposed by his employers. His original idea was to build high above the river front on the lines of Somerset House, with a splendid open processional way leading from the Parliament to Buckingham Palace. The plan would have enhanced the central importance of Parliament, but it would have dwarfed Westminster Hall, for which generations of parliamentarians express, without any conscious analysis, a profound admiration. Barry demonstrated a bold self-confidence by offering to raise the Hall's venerable hammer-beamed roof which still evokes the memory of Richard II. Nobody was willing to authorize so audacious an idea; besides it would have cost more than Parliament was willing to pay.

The government of the day, Melbourne's second ministry, did not have the foresight to allow the architect the ample space and hard ground needed for the new Parliament. Instead he was confined to a swampy triangle of ground at the extreme edge of the river bank, occasionally below the level of high tide. The soil under a large part of the site was the same as the river bed, exceedingly treacherous and in places little better than quicksand. The Duke of Wellington was supposed to have advised that the construction should, on military grounds, have its back to the water, to prevent infiltration by a hostile mob. But what was strategically sound was architecturally a costly folly; a watery quagmire is not a sure foundation on which to place an immense building. This should have been obvious to the legislators and Ministers who directed Barry, but they did not appreciate this elementary fact. The architect went ahead with an enormous coffer-dam – a box filled with stone and concrete behind which dredging was to take place and foundations laid. It was intended to draw the piles of the coffer-dam but in view of the strength of the tideway and the threat that the scour of the river might undermine the foundations, Barry ordered the piles to be cut off level with the river bed, leaving the lower part of the dam as an outwork below the main river wall, which he faced with large blocks of Aberdeen granite. Behind this wall, foundations were laid upon concrete, which in places was twelve feet thick.

By now the site contained a vast raft floating on a lake of mud, on which the largest building in Britain was to be raised. Four years had passed since the competition was won. It was not until 1840 that the foundation stone was laid, and already no great officer of state wished to be associated with the hazardous project. On 27 April the first stone was laid by the architect's wife. She at least demonstrated her confidence in her husband's skill.

After the laying of the foundation stone, it might have been thought that the work would go ahead, but the obstructions to progress had hardly begun. There were still old parts of the original Palace of Westminster which the fire had damaged but not wholly destroyed, and these were soon re-occupied by their former users, whose deliberations had to be accorded priority. The Painted Chamber in which the Lords and Commons had met for the opening of Parliament since 1341 was retained by the Lords as their debating chamber for seven years after the laying of the foundation stone of the new Palace. It was the room in which the death warrant of King Charles I was signed, and was reputed to be the bedroom in which Edward the Confessor died in 1066. It was not until 1847 that Barry was able to complete its demolition.

Another obstruction in the way of the new Palace was the Court of Requests adjoining the Painted Chamber at the south end of Westminster Hall. It was the original banqueting hall of the old Palace and later became the court in which petitions to the King were heard. After the fire, the Court of Requests was fitted out as a temporary debating chamber for the Commons who met there until 1852, when it too was demolished. Finally there was St Stephen's Hall, the old royal chapel of St Stephen, where since 1547 the Commons had sat. There was an attempt to retain it after the fire, but its walls were so clearly unsafe that the architect was permitted to pull it down and re-erect a new hall in its place, not however as a debating chamber but out of a deference to antiquity for its own sake, for which he had no personal predilection.

CHAPTER THREE

TALENT ON THE CHEAP

1839

Barry's brilliance as a large-scale planner was already recognized by the government of the day. In 1840 he was invited to suggest improvements to Trafalgar Square, so that not only Parliament itself, but the principal approach from the centre of London should be in harmony with the new plans. Half a mile to the north of Parliament, the National Gallery's frontage is that of a single-storey Palladian villa with a portico of Greco-Roman pillars. It is a relatively insignificant and unhappily proportioned building which occupies the finest site in the capital, with the land below sloping away to Whitehall and the river. In an attempt to improve its setting, a plan had been prepared for raising the whole square to the level of the pavement outside the National Gallery with a balustrade at the lower edge of the square. Barry pointed out that this would not enhance but further diminish the impact of the National Gallery's façade; his advice was to leave the level of the square sloping down to Cockspur Street, but to construct a terrace below and near the front of the gallery which would appear part of the building, thus increasing instead of reducing its height.

This plan was adopted, but its effect was largely spoiled by the erection of the Nelson column, a piece of disproportionate absurdity against which Barry protested vehemently. To use columns as pedestals for statues was contrary to his sense of architectural merit, and in this case was doubly objectionable because the column cut in two the front of the gallery and interfered with a grand flight of steps which he contemplated would lead down from the centre of his terrace, as wide as the portico of the Gallery and appearing from a distance to be part of it.

The frustration of his full scheme for Trafalgar Square was symptomatic of official dealings with Barry. In middle life he was still vigorous, impulsive and energetic, but those who dealt with him were well aware that he had had little schooling and virtually no professional training, except for his six teenage years with Messrs Middleton & Bailey in their modest premises in Paradise Row, Lambeth. The government, while accepting his talent and imagination, felt that duty required them to remind him of his humble place in the established order of the Queen's Works, and to grant rather less than was customary in the case of a major architect.

The question arose of whether Barry should be paid the regular professional remuneration of 5 per cent commission on the outlay of the work – which for some years had been normal practice – or whether his services should be paid on a lower scale.

Expenditure on public works had been under parliamentary scrutiny and criticism for some years. It was Barry's misfortune that his payment was decided at the end of a long series of near-scandals. In 1828 Henry Bankes MP had moved in the House for an account of the salaries and commissions paid to architects attached to the Office of Works and the Commissioner, Sir Benjamin Stephenson, had to defend his department against charges of architectural extravagance. One Member (George Ellis) declared that 'the attached Architects are expensive and worse than useless, as they prevent competition and thereby occasion expensive as well as hideous buildings'. No doubt he had in mind the upkeep of George IV's Brighton Pavilion, which was an annual drain of several thousand pounds on the taxpayer. By 1828 the architect Nash had spent half a million pounds on enlarging and remodelling Buckingham Palace, although his estimate for the work three years earlier had been for £200000.

Against this background of carping but sometimes well-founded criticism, it was not surprising that the mistakes of the past led the

Office of Works to decide on a lump-sum payment to Barry, instead of the usual percentage commission. Sir Benjamin Stephenson's advocacy of this method of payment was the deciding factor, and the Treasury endorsed both the principle and the amount proposed, based on Stephenson's reckoning of 3 per cent of the original estimate of £800000 and officially described at the time as 'fair and liberal'.

In every age there have been among the Members of the Commons those who have seen themselves as the tribunes of the people. They are the men who, in their own estimation, see further than their colleagues and who are quickest at perceiving unnecessary expenditure, futile delay or downright waste. Unfortunately Charles Barry fell an easy victim to the attacks of such publicists. Prince Albert himself, in the context of work for Buckingham Palace, set a certain standard by agreeing that Thomas Cubitt was 'the safest and cheapest man we deal with' since he was charging only 5s. 9d. a day for skilled men and 3s. 6d. for labourers. Barry, with 1200 to 1400 workers, mainly engaged by his excellent contractors Grissell & Peto, did not aim at getting recognition of the new Palace by saving candle ends.

Inevitably, the architect's grandiose designs for rebuilding Parliament evoked hostility at a time of financial stringency. The revenue was falling and income tax had been re-introduced. Even the Queen felt it her duty to pay although she was advised that constitutionally she need not do so. The new rate was 7d. in the £. Parliament and the public could see for themselves the dilatory character of work on the new building. The masons working on the river front were on strike from 1841 to 1843. One method of keeping down expenses was obvious: 'to pay the architect as little as possible, as infrequently as possible, and with as much fuss as possible'.

Barry's negotiating position was weakened by his eagerness to begin work on the assumption that good faith would be shown by the government. As it turned out, his trust was seriously abused. Queen Victoria's government was no more scrupulous in financial matters than any of its successors. Although finance to begin the work had been voted by the Commons in July 1837, there was no specific arrangement for paying the architect. It was not until March

1839, more than nineteen months after the work on the building began, that a Treasury minute was issued rejecting the idea of paying the architect the normal commission and stating that 'in deference to the opinions expressed at different times in both Houses against the principle of remunerating architects by a commission or percentage upon the amount of their estimates' and considering 'the extent and importance of the building and the very large expenditure contemplated in Mr Barry's estimate', the sum of £25 000 was decided upon.

On receiving this decision, which was endorsed by Lord Bessborough as Treasury Minister, Barry first asked to be informed of the principle on which the amount had been decided, but this request was refused by the Office of Works (temporarily combined with the Commission of Woods and Forests), the Department of State responsible for handing down the Treasury's *ukase*. The best that Barry could do, bearing in mind that after two years' building he had nothing yet above ground level, was to bow to the decision under protest: 'I cannot,' he wrote, 'in justice to myself and the profession to which I belong, refrain from expressing most decidedly my opinion that the amount is very inadequate to the great labour and responsibility that will devolve upon me in the superintendence, direction and completion of the intended edifice', and he trusted that, when the work was further advanced, the Department might award him 'the remainder of the remuneration which has hitherto been customary on similar occasions'. No rejoinder was made to this letter, and in January 1841 Barry wrote again to the Office of Works suggesting that the making out of accounts and measuring the work executed should be borne by the Department, and not by himself, in view of his low fee. The Office of Works in a cursory reply ruled that these costs must be borne by him. The whole matter then remained in abeyance for eight years, until a point was reached in the construction at which Barry felt he could reasonably hark back to the unanswered letter which he wrote to the Office of Works in 1839, in which he had expressed the hope that the normal architect's fee might be considered appropriate, if the work should prove satisfactory to the public at large.

It was thought by Barry that the fixed fee decided on by the

Treasury in 1839, if it ever had any legal validity, was now vitiated by the entire change from the circumstances on which it was first based – especially the assumption that the whole building would be completed in six years. Accordingly he wrote in February 1849 – ten years after the original settlement – reminding the government that in 1839 he had only acceded to Lord Bessborough's fixed fee conditionally and under protest. His argument would, of course, have been far stronger if in 1839 he had refused to accept £25 000 on the ground that it was contrary to the normal practice of paying architects' fees. But at that time, after overcoming the difficulties of the site, opposition by rivals and fierce criticism of his successful plans, he felt he was not strongly placed to fight an adamant decision of the Treasury. His enemies would gladly have seized the opportunity afforded by a breach between himself and the government, especially on a subject on which public opinion was certainly divided. He was always hopeful that the absence of an answer to his first letter of acceptance under protest indicated at least a tacit acquiescence by the government in the force of his argument. Vainly Barry argued that by 1849 'between 8000 and 9000 original drawings and models have been made, a large proportion from my own hand and the remainder under my immediate supervision'. Successive governments repeated the first high-handed rejection of his requests for a revised fee, and refused him the opportunity to put his case to an arbitrator.

By this time the building had advanced to a point at which the great men who had been so reluctant to be associated with failure became ready and indeed anxious to have their names linked with success. Public attention had been drawn to the opportunities, so long apparent to Barry, of constructing a new palace worthy of the times. The Prince Consort, always ready to intervene with helpful advice, frequently visited the work and saw the show-window which it would provide for the arts of painting and sculpture. Accordingly a Royal Commission (the Fine Arts Commission) was appointed in November 1841, under the chairmanship of the Prince Consort, to superintend the distribution of works of art, painting and sculpture, and to say what should appear and where it should appear. Membership of this Commission was obviously to be both an honour and a privilege. It included the Duke of Sutherland, the

Marquess of Lansdowne, the Earls of Lincoln, Shrewsbury and Aberdeen, Viscount Palmerston and Viscount Melbourne, Sir Robert Peel, Lord John Russell, the Speaker of the House of Commons (the Rt Hon. Charles Shaw Lefevre) and many other men of eminence. Inevitably, in the tenor of the times, it did not include Barry or his brilliant assistant, Pugin, who was particularly concerned with interior decoration.

Barry regarded his exclusion as a slight, but cooperated to the full in attempting to interest the Commission in the progress and plans of his architectural work, and it was to the Commission that he addressed his plea for a revision of his remuneration. On neither point did he receive any effective help; his practical suggestions were passed over, and his long and well-argued case for the normal architect's fee received no answer whatever. Already it was recognized that in this new building there was an architectural masterpiece in the making, with half a million pounds being estimated for the furniture, fixtures and interior decoration.

It should not have needed Barry's advocacy to convince the Royal Commission that if paintings and sculpture were to be valuable additions to his own decorative plans, they should be in harmony with their surroundings. Such common-sense ideas were not imported into decisions of the Commission. Barry suggested that the bare and dreary condition of Westminster Hall might be relieved by statues raised on pedestals in shallow niches close to the walls; they would be surmounted by enriched canopies and divided by paintings. The Commission ignored this proposal and decided to place a double row of statues prominently throughout the length of the narrow St Stephen's Hall, distorting its proportions by their height and without any relation to the background paintings. The intention was to represent the great orators, Pitt, Fox and the rest, gesturing in mid-rhetoric; they stand to this day, over-sized effigies which spoil the architectural effect of St Stephen's Hall and seriously diminish the impact of the Central Lobby. After his father's death, the Rev. Alfred Barry wrote: 'These things ought not to have been, and it is hardly possible that they should have taken place, had the Commission included one member who had before his eyes the building as a whole, and the scale and succession of its various parts.'

Two more monumental follies of Prince Albert's Commission may be mentioned. The Royal Gallery was to be filled with paintings relating to 'the military and naval glory of the country'. Two vast tableaux by Daniel Maclise were chosen – the mounted Wellington shaking hands with Blücher after the latter's bloody pursuit of Napoleon following Waterloo, and Captain Hardy cradling the dying Nelson on the deck of his flagship *Victory* during the battle of Trafalgar. So big are these pictures that it is hardly possible to view each as a whole, and a contemporary joke was that the great Gallery, which was not in Barry's original plan, had to be built to accommodate them.

A further egregious error concerned the fine ante-chamber of the House of Lords, known as the Prince's Chamber. Portraits 'relating to the Tudor family' were to be placed here, and for good measure include Lady Jane Grey, Mary, Queen of Scots, Darnley and the six wives of Henry VIII. They were duly installed, but so high that at fifteen feet their features are difficult to discern. The place of honour was given to a cumbrous statue of Queen Victoria by Gibson, suitable perhaps for a public park but utterly out of place in Pugin's gracious ante-room.

Pugin's frenetic activity in Barry's service was spared one threatened frustration. The Royal Commission began to assume the superintendence of architectural details and to invite competitions for the best work in wood carving, metal work and stained glass. They even moved into a laborious examination of the various methods and styles of painting in fresco, oil, encaustic or water-glass, and then, finding themselves getting too deeply involved, the Commission stepped back and reported that 'experience proved that it was on many accounts advisable to leave with the architect the responsibility of all strictly decorative works', importing however a note of surprise that hitherto 'he had undertaken on his own responsibility the whole of the decorative works except the stained glass', and implying that though this was slightly in excess of his authorized field, they were now disclaiming all responsibility except for 'works of art'.

The Commission decided to illustrate great epochs in constitutional, social and ecclesiastical history from Saxon times to the acquisition of the Empire. Pugin's art held no special interest for them since he was Barry's man, now formally appointed superintendent of wood carving. It was more than ordinary cooperation which Barry expected of him. 'With no tools but a rule and a rough pencil, amidst a continuous rattle of marvellous stories, slashing criticisms and shouts of laughter, Pugin would get through an amount of good work which astonished us,' wrote J. L. Wolfe, Barry's close friend. Every drawing was supervised by Barry, yet Pugin's origin- ality and enthusiasm, even in its eccentricities, was inspiring and irresistible. The same could hardly be said of the somewhat jejune pictures of scenes from English history, approved by the Commission. One of E. M. Ward's eight painstaking frescoes in the corridor leading from the Central Lobby to the Commons Chamber shows Charles II landing at Dover in 1660 and being welcomed with a fluttering Union Jack.

Pugin's appointment was used by the Treasury in an attempt to diminish still further the sum payable to Barry as his professional remuneration, when it was suggested that Pugin's salary of £200 a year should be paid by Barry out of the fixed sum awarded him in 1839 – fifteen years earlier – since Pugin had relieved the architect of much work on interior decoration. As Pugin had died in 1852, this post mortem attempt to penalize Barry was too much for even his patience. He put the argument contained in his unanswered letters to successive governments in the hands of a leading solicitor, John Meadows White.

White succeeded, after a further delay of six months, in meeting the Minister representing the Office of Works, James Wilson MP, and strongly pressing Barry's claim to the normal architect's commission of 5 per cent. By this time the cost of works had risen to one and a half million pounds, and the original fixed sum of £25 000 was so totally unrelated to that new figure that the Treasury grudgingly agreed to 3 per cent on the outlay instead of the fixed sum, and to 1 per cent for the architect's staff and their expenses. Barry still argued that the allowance hitherto made to architects for all public buildings was 5 per cent. The Treasury, now impatient at the delayed settlement, responded by ordering Barry to undertake to complete the building at the rate they had laid down, as a condition of any futher payments, and refusing him a reference of his claim to arbitration. It was a shabby forced settlement which Barry never forgot, and for which he took later a certain degree of revenge by withholding all his architect's drawings of the new Parliament buildings, a loss calculated to cause embarrassment for the government and headaches for future architects during the whole of the building's life.

There was little else which Barry could do. With the benefit of modern legislation, a servant of the Crown can today sue for recovery of a payment due to him from the government, but in the nineteenth century such payments were a matter of favour, not of right. The original fee was based on an expectation that the building would take six years to complete; but it took six years from the date of the fire before the foundation stone was laid. Twenty years later, Barry's death did not mark the finish of the building, and his son, Edward, worked on for ten more years (1860–70) before the New Palace was complete. The son, however, was paid the customary architect's fee of 5 per cent without argument.

CHAPTER FOUR

INTOLERABLE
INTERFERENCE

1840

Public interest in the new Palace of Westminster brought with it a host of official mosquitoes, whose activities were to drive Barry almost to distraction. Different authorities were appointed to superintend each section of the work, and soon the architect found that though he was responsible for progress he was in no position to control it, since his own authority was inevitably much less than that of his controllers. His own character inclined to the choleric, and though he was open to suggestions, he was alert and ready to resist dictation. The first clash occurred when an expert was brought in to improve upon the known principles of circulating air and warmth in the interior of a large building. He was Dr David Boswell Reid, a Scottish teacher of chemistry, and it is typical of government planning that his appointment in January 1840 was made without consulting the architect. His duty was to make provision for ventilation and heating, and his plans for the House of Commons in their temporary Chamber had succeeded. Sceptics suggested that the Reid system, which had worked well for one chamber, would not necessarily be applicable on a vast scale to the new building which was to contain 1100 rooms.

As the Rev. Alfred Barry wrote, in measured criticism seven years after his father's death, 'No one can question the right of the House of Lords and Commons to examine, censure and indirectly control those who are in their service. But then these public servants should be left free from other interference, with undivided power and undivided responsibility. This was not the case with Mr Barry.... No architect in his senses is likely to refuse advice. . . . But to divide power is to paralyse action and destroy responsibility.'

Dr Reid, as Barry's first and major opponent, had some brilliant ideas for the new Palace of Westminster. All chimneys were to be dispensed with – a novel and splendid innovation in a London already drowning in seas of smoking chimney pots. All the smoke from the eighty tons of coal burned weekly in open grates during the winter was to be carried into great shafts forming mock turrets in the external design. Beneath the turrets, large furnaces were to burn in order to maintain a constant upward draught. Other shafts were designed to draw in and disperse the cold air, to improve immeasurably the system of ventilation and to make the debating chambers and other public rooms warm in winter and cool in summer. Ingenious screens below the Terrace level imposed a handicap upon the foggy breath of the river; its air had first to penetrate layers of cotton wool before being drawn into the ventilation system. Other screens, saturated with water, were ready to combat the hazards of inordinately hot weather, and below Big Ben a great fire drove upwards and outwards the legislators' own hot air from the Commons Chamber.

With Barry and Reid working independently towards different goals, division and disagreement might have been anticipated. Between floors, for example, Dr Reid looked for an 18-foot hollow space, and the central tower itself, 300 feet in height and 75 feet across, was inserted into the original plans on the insistence of Dr Reid that he needed a central ventilating shaft as well as the towers at each end of the building.

These pseudo-scientific plans delighted the Commons, as in a later generation, after the bombing in 1941, did the complicated arrangements for cooling the reconstructed Chamber, which involved visual inspection through a periscope by a Works official concealed below the floor. Dr Reid's grotesque shafts had more than one disadvantage. A vast empty space under the Central Tower, on which he insisted, required the lowering of the fine roof of the Central Lobby, soon to be encumbered by the Fine Arts Commission's street-size statues. No limits were put on Dr Reid's requirements of accommodation in space and position. Barry believed in light and air, with spacious rooms and large windows, and was an early exponent of double-glazing when appropriate, as in the House of Lords Chamber. Dr Reid maintained his preference for enclosed channels of air between floors, under the roofs and within dividing walls, beginning at river level, percolating through the building and eventually floating out through the topmost towers. It was a sprightly and superficial idea to apply to the most important building in Britain, and completely contrary to the principles of fire-proofing which were being simultaneously laid down by the Office of Works. It should have been clear that internal draughts for air would also serve admirably to stimulate a local outbreak of fire into an all-enveloping blanket of flames; even in a later modified form the system drew in the stench of the sullied Thames and sent gusts of unsavoury kitchen smells from the basement of the Speaker's House directly into the Ministers' rooms and corridors near the Commons Chamber.

It might be asked why Barry did not stop the folly before it developed, but an architect is in the hands of his clients, and if the clients insist he must eventually yield to their wishes or abandon the work for which he has been commissioned. The clients at the Commons end of the building were pleased with Dr Reid, and the architect had at first to wait upon events. In retrospect it is easy to see the faults in what was the first primitive attempt at air-conditioning a large public building. There were underlying reasons for the exceptional tolerance of the Commons towards the vagaries of their ventilation expert. Dr Reid displayed much solicitude for the health of Members, at a time when the subject was one of real anxiety. The new Parliament was being built in a grossly insanitary and overcrowded central area, in which disease was spreading as fast as the population increased. The stench in the streets and in the atmosphere within the walls of Parliament was unbearable, and therefore any new theory promising to bring relief was uncritically welcomed. It was believed that cholera, which was then causing many thousands of deaths each year, was transmitted by polluted air and poor ventilation. The miasma which arose from heaps of filth was considered to be the main danger, and to purify the air was therefore essential to combat the infection.

To meet Dr Reid's requirements, alterations became necessary in every part of the new Palace until it appeared that one-third of the whole cubic capacity of the building was to be surrendered to the needs of built-in ventilation cavities. For a long time the Commons retained their belief in the ingenious doctor, only beginning to doubt his methods when he exploded gunpowder in the roof cavity to demonstrate his ventilating skills. At this point, after nearly five years of increasing frustration, the disagreement between the architect and the ventilator broke out publicly in a torrent of controversy and mutual recrimination.

It was not without significance, in view of the government's subsequent refusal to submit the issue of Barry's fee to arbitration, that they decided to submit the argument between himself and Dr Reid to professional arbitration, and that the arbitrator they chose, Joseph Gwilt, came down wholly on Barry's side of the case. It would perhaps be difficult not to sympathize a little with Dr Reid when he read Gwilt's conclusions in September 1845, five and a half years after the remarkable experiments in ventilation had been started under his bold direction. The arbitrator reported that the vertical flues destroyed the fireproof character of the building, that he could find no detailed drawings to explain the requirements of Dr Reid's system, that the delays in building were due to the division of authority, and that total control should be restored to the architect, provided he called in and acted on the advice of some experts in ventilation.

On receiving news of this highly critical report, Dr Reid decided to resist the decision of the government's arbitrator by petitioning the Lords and Commons separately. This was an astute move calculated to split the two Houses into two camps and further discursive delay, and in this he was not unsuccessful. His petitions had to be considered by Committees in each House, and witnesses had to be called and examined at length on whether the system of ventilation had to be applied to the whole building or whether it was practicable and advisable to ventilate the two parts separately. Another year passed before a Lords Committee reported that the warming and ventilating of their House at least should be confided to Barry, and from 1846 Dr Reid ceased to have any responsibility for the building as a whole. The attempted division of authority between the two Houses was found to be impracticable and Barry was left in general charge, with advice on ventilation being given him by Professor Faraday; and some constructional changes were made to the eccentric system of Dr Reid.

The changes were authorized too late for all the faults to be remedied. Barry was blamed for unsatisfactory ventilation in parts of the Commons and the ventilation and lighting of that House were restored to Dr Reid, whose main support had always come from the Lower House. Soon, however, the patience of the Commons ran out, and Reid was at last superseded by Goldsworthy Gurney, whose first task was to set aside the hazardous system of collecting all smoke into one shaft. The central tower capped by a tapering spire remains a graceful tribute to the Doctor's six years of exasperating experimentation. The great purposeless ventilating vault above the roof of the Central Lobby is still unused and unseen, except by an occasional pigeon which makes its way inside for shelter in inclement weather.

The debate, however, and the bitterness engendered between the Lords' support of Barry and the Commons' hankering after Reid has left a permanent mark on the structure of the Commons Chamber, and emphasized a more than theoretical division between the Houses.

In February 1847 the new House of Lords was occupied for the first time; some early complaints were made about its acoustics, but as soon as the Lords got accustomed to speaking in their new Chamber, they found nothing that was seriously wrong with its design. Meanwhile the Commons, still mindful of the clash leading to the extrusion of Dr Reid by the architect, regarded the change from their temporary Chamber, in which they had sat since the fire, with misgivings. The Court of Requests in Old Palace Yard had served them well enough after it had been re-modelled with four tiers of seats running down each wall and facing inwards, on the principle of the old St Stephen's Chapel. The Commons first sat in the new Chamber designed for them by Barry on 30 May 1850, and immediately they found fault with what he had so painstakingly prepared. In Members' opinion, the Chamber was all wrong and inferior to the temporary house which had proved very convenient. Barry's original design had been for a spacious debating hall with ample accommodation for over 600 Members as well as for the public. In the course of construction, however, the authorities of the House, bearing in mind the smaller scale of their former meeting place in St Stephen's Chapel, required Barry to reduce the size of his plan and to restrict the accommodation for the public. Yet as soon as Members saw that it was smaller they expressed vehement dissatisfaction.

Not for the last time had the authorities misjudged the temper of the House. For example, the Ladies' Gallery was neither large nor convenient, but it was only with great difficulty that Barry had earlier obtained consent for accommodating women visitors at all. In the Building Committee in 1835 Lord Brougham had spoken on the admission of ladies, expressing what had then been taken as the general feeling in both Houses: 'If such a proposition is to be made, I enter my protest against it, and shall take the sense of your lordships upon it, as being contrary to the principle which ought to govern legislative proceedings. I think the ladies would be better employed in almost any other way, than in attending parliamentary debates. I like to see them in their proper places.' Ignoring the probably counterfeit sincerity of this declaration, the Marquess of Lansdowne added: 'Ladies are not mentioned in the Report and, so far as I can prevent it, they never shall be.'

When at length the House of Commons met, with an attendance greatly increased by public excitement and curiosity, the unfortunate architect was criticized for lack of accommodation in the Lobbies and Galleries. It was easier at this point for the House authorities, the Speaker, the Clerk and the Serjeant at Arms, who had no special interest one way or the other, to remain silent and let blame fall on the architect rather than to admit he had followed their explicit directions. Members had been used to a low ceiling in the temporary House and their next complaint was that the ceiling was too high and that they had difficulty in hearing.

Barry felt that the new Chamber should be given a fair trial. He knew that speech can be adjusted to space more easily than space to speeches, and that inaudibility is not invariably the fault of the auditorium. But there was no fair trial to be had; he was imperatively ordered to lower the ceiling, and the only way this could be done was by introducing a false ceiling with sloping sides, cutting the windows in half and ruining the proportions of the room. Never could an architect have carried out work more unwillingly. Generations to come would look on the House of Commons Chamber as the very centre of the new building, and most would at first entry find it disappointingly cramped and unworthy of its purpose. Barry would have fully agreed. When the alterations had been reluctantly made, a beautifully carved wooden ceiling and tall stained glass windows were among the features sacrificed; he no longer considered the House his own work. He would never speak of it or even enter it unless it was absolutely necessary. Meanwhile the Members emphasized their disapproval of Barry's original design by going back to the Court of Requests until the changes were completed. They did not settle permanently in their new Chamber till 3 February 1852, five years later than the Lords.

Ironically this section of the building, so distasteful to Barry after the alterations enforced on him by the Commons, became so closely associated with his name that when German bombs destroyed the Commons Chamber on 10 May 1941, the Prime Minister, Winston Churchill, declared with an emotional gesture that it must be replaced entirely as it was.

Subsequent research showed that Parliament's concern with ventilation was to some extent misplaced. Even Chadwick, who published his report on the Sanitary Conditions of the Labouring Population in 1842, did not accept the true theory that water polluted by excreta caused the outbreaks of the twin scourges, cholera and typhoid fever. The exhalations from filthy sewers were, however, already a topic of current anxiety. Disputes over the drainage system for the new building involved Barry and Reid in yet another controversy.

The sewer constructed for the new Houses in 1838–9 by the contractors to the Westminster Court of Sewers had been large and brick-built. By 1848 the development of sanitary engineering under the impetus of Chadwick had produced a glazed earthenware pipe which could be efficiently flushed. Henry Austin, who was consulting engineer to the Metropolitan Sewers Commission, criticized the earlier work and urged the substitution of a nine-inch glazed pipe. Barry indignantly rebutted the criticism, throwing the blame on Dr Reid. Not unexpectedly, this additional dispute came before Parliament. In 1850 the main sewer was altered and the outfall of the parliamentary sewage was discharged into the Thames, just before Westminster Bridge; consequently Parliament's unwise decision led to the entire waste with its accompanying odours drifting back on the incoming tide to lap against the Terrace wall.

CHAPTER FIVE

THE HARROW OF
CRITICISM

1845

Criticisms of the new building and conflicting views on its merits occupied more and more of the time of both Members of Parliament and the architect through investigation by Select Committees of each House. Day after day and year after year Charles Barry was summoned to explain himself and justify his activities.

Select Committees in the nineteenth century were not, as a cynic later defined them, little gatherings of the unwilling, picked from the unfit, to do the unnecessary. Instead they were composed of a dozen or more leading Members determined, within the limits of their social engagements, to get at the truth by tireless questioning of this or that witness. And the witness was supposed to defer to the greater percipience of his interrogators, leaving them at leisure to prepare a critical report on all aspects of problems which seemed to threaten extravagance in public funds or to reveal any cause for concern. A great deal of the delay in building the new Parliament must be attributed to the work of almost interminable Select Committees of each House, which sat in judgement on the architect.

The form of examination is almost unchanged today, except that in the past few years the press and public have been invited to watch the witnesses being questioned. At the outset of each inquiry the Committee meets in private and, in the official phrase, deliberates. The main purpose of the deliberation is to choose the Chairman, whose name has already been privately indicated to the Members by the party whips. In theory the election is untrammelled, but in practice the Member concerned will have been approached by the whips to ascertain his willingness to serve. John Grant, a young and keen Member of the 1970s, describes in his book how he arrived for the first sitting of his Committee just too late to take part in the election of his Chairman, but comments on the choice as uninspiring, presumably not one he would have supported had he been punctual. The episode throws light on one admirable feature of the system – the sittings invariably begin at the precise time for which Members are summoned to attend. No Chairman in the whole history of the committee system has been known to be late. The Commons has imported into its proceedings, dating perhaps from the period of the great clock controversy, what amounts to a pathological concern with time. Uproar may be overlooked, but it is a matter of the gravest concern if the rules for beginning or concluding a sitting are disregarded by so much as a single minute.

After the process of deliberating in private is over, the witness, who has been waiting uneasily in the corridor outside the committee room, is called in and asked to take the witness's chair, which is placed in the centre of the room facing the half-moon of Members' seats and directly opposite the official shorthand writer. Beyond him, in the centre of the half-moon, sits the Chairman of the Committee. The Chairman usually opens a public hearing with a series of acute and highly relevant questions. Nine times out of ten these slick questions will have been supplied to the Chairman privately after diligent research and inquiries by the Clerk to the Committee, with perhaps a little homework by the Chairman himself. This, of course, is never revealed to the witness, who has a ready defence, however, by giving answers of such extreme technicality that the Chairman is unable to follow the explanation. Another defence may be brevity. Charles Barry was sometimes brusque in his answers and capable of responding with a sharp 'No', giving the impression of impatience and an unwillingness to suffer fools gladly. Obsequious assent, so gratifying to Members' self-esteem, was never forthcoming. As he wrote to Pugin after one long session: 'I am in a towering rage and in the right humour for throwing up my appointment at the New

Palace of Westminster, which I expect I shall be driven to do before long. All the arrangements of the new House of Commons, including the form, size, proportions, taste and everything else concerning it are in abeyance, and awaiting the fiat of a Committee of the House of Commons, of all tribunals the most unfit to decide.'

At the end of each day's inquisition, the shorthand writer, who has been sitting in front of the Chairman silently recording the questions and answers, sends a transcript to the printer, and in due course a blue book of the evidence is published, together with the report of the Committee to the House. The Committee has no executive power, beyond sending for witnesses, and the House itself may or may not take action or even any notice of a Select Committee. Once a report has been laid upon the Table of the House, the Committee may have no further function. Yet this is the system which was brought to maturity by the parliamentarians of the nineteenth century and which, with a few refinements, has occupied hundreds of hours of Members' time in the modern Parliament. The examination of great national problems, leading eventually to legislation, is what Select Committees aspire to achieve, and they have occasionally succeeded; but the other demands on Members' time makes a Select Committee unsuitable for long and complicated inquiries. Instead the great issues are referred to Royal Commissions, to departmental inquiries, or even to meetings of party executives. It has been left for Select Committees to inquire into more detailed matters, and especially into domestic items affecting the daily life of Members within the walls of Parliament. In these questions Members have revelled, expressing all the frustrations and disappointments of their national role in criticizing the discomforts of the building and the inefficiency of those who serve but dare not, in the main, answer back. Membership of a Select Committee is a consolation for those hundreds of private Members who would otherwise have no particular function in the machinery of Parliament, and who might spend even more time importuning Ministers on behalf of their constituents or on outside interests. It was this mighty procedural octopus with which Barry slowly became more and more entangled, and which Pugin, through the subordinate character of his employment, managed entirely to escape.

In March and in May of 1844 Barry was summoned by a Select Committee of the House of Lords to give evidence on the slow rate of progress in their building. In June he was called in and examined by a Select Committee of the Commons. The interrogation in the Commons lasted hours, covering every aspect of the work. In the 85th question, Viscount Duncan challenged the architect: 'You stated in 1836 that in about six years you anticipated the entire completion of the building?'

To this Barry could only reply: 'It was perhaps very unwise of me to give that answer, as there were so many contingencies upon which the completion of the building depends. It was, however, a mere conjecture.'

Some Members were friendly. Sir Robert Inglis asked: 'In the whole progress of the work, have you not had to consider the necessity of combining the actual sitting of the two Houses in something like their present locality, with the progress of the work surrounding them? Has that been the reason why there has been a difficulty on your part in stating the precise period at which the whole work might be considered finished?'

Barry readily conceded that was one of the difficulties, and he agreed with his sympathetic questioner that he had not caused the interruption of the business of Parliament for a single day.

'Of course,' went on the questioner, 'if you had erected this building in any other portion of London, in a clear space, its progress might have been determined more accurately and at all events completed more rapidly?'

'Unquestionably,' replied Barry.

By question 159, he was describing the principle of fire-proofing by using iron for the roofs, protected from rust by the application of zinc, but always having to defend the cost incurred. Would lead have been cheaper? No. Copper? Much dearer. How thick was the plate? The thickness of the iron plating was three sixteenths of an inch. Thirty questions later, the witness was delivering a comparative statement of the space allocated to gallery seats for peers, allowing twenty inches in width, compared with strangers in the public gallery at eighteen inches.

A week later, Barry was back again for more questions, having

in the meantime conferred on the arrangements in the Commons
with the Speaker, the Clerk of the House and the Serjeant at Arms.
Were they each satisfied with the details affecting their responsibilities? Yes, they replied, provided they were not to be held totally
responsible for what was barely within their scope.

Then came Dr David Boswell Reid, with his lengthy pseudo-
scientific exposition in terms well calculated to flatter the sensibili-
ties of Members. On ventilation in the debating chamber, the doctor
declared: 'In all I now refer to I speak of special cases, where perhaps
a slight illness or peculiarity of temperament, or of the circumstances of the moment render local adaptations desirable; the alteration of the circulation in individual constitutions, as the evening
advances, as it is more remote from the period of dinner for instance,
or from the period at which any Member may have been addressing
the House, the amount of excitement, and many other causes, tend
very materially not only to affect the feelings, supposing the state
of the atmosphere to continue without change; but the extent to
which the condition of the air itself is modified by such circumstances, varies with the condition to which the frame may have been
reduced by previous exhaustion. Thus Members who may have
found any particular atmosphere exceedingly agreeable at one hour,
may find the same air very uncomfortable at another, from changes
which have taken place, not in the air, but in their own frame.'

When asked about the excessive amount of space he was taking
up with his ventilation schemes, he took the chance of a side-swipe
at the architect: the vaults in the river front before Reid entered on
any duties or had anything to do with the ventilation 'would have
been filled up with rubbish, had I not represented that it would form
a magnificent series of vaults for cooling the atmosphere in sultry
weather, the greatest difficulties in conducting the ventilation always
occurring then'.

By 4 July Barry was summoned again in front of the Committee,
the questions to himself and other witnesses having now reached
over 700.

In August he was recalled to the Upper House to answer some
sharp questions from a House of Lords Select Committee. On 8
August the Earl of Shaftesbury as Chairman asked: 'Were you

directed by the Office of Works to prepare drawings for the finishings of the House of Lords?'

Barry's patience was wearing thin and his responses became shorter. 'No,' he replied.

'Then why do you wait for instructions now?'

'Because,' said Barry, 'I think it better, after the late misunderstanding as to authority, not to proceed without authority in anything.'

Shaftesbury: 'You have been told by Committees of both Houses that it would be extremely desirable to have the Committee rooms proceeded with as fast as possible, have you not?'

Barry: 'I am not aware that I have.'

Shaftesbury: 'Did you know that it was the desire of both Houses that the Committee rooms should be finished as quickly as possible?'

Barry: 'I happen to know that is the wish of individual Members of both Houses. I shall not make any alteration except by express authority.'

Shaftesbury: 'No suggestion, therefore, coming from any mere parliamentary authority such as Officers of the House, will be attended to?'

Barry: 'No.'

The deference had gone, and defence was becoming defiance. But it was then that Barry went down to Brighton to recover from illness and sent a cry of despair to Augustus Welby Pugin to come back and help him: '. . . It is of vital importance to me that the fittings and decorations of the House of Lords should be finished with the utmost possible dispatch.'

Throughout 1845 Barry was brought under the harrow of criticism from each House but more particularly by Select Committees of the House of Lords. The slowness of the work and the delays in getting into their new chamber were extremely annoying to the Members of the Upper House, particularly as the Commons, thanks in part to Reid's successful ventilation, were beginning to grow accustomed and indeed to like their temporary chamber in the old Court of Requests immediately facing the outer walls of the new House of Lords. The impression was growing, as Prince Albert and his Fine Arts Commission were giving so much more attention to gilding Pugin's lilies in the new rooms and halls of the peers, that Barry was not their man at all. Nothing in fact was further from the truth. Barry's answers to the Lords were increasingly brief, but among the peers there were a few who did not fail to recognize that they were dealing with a creative and exceptionally gifted man, whereas his critics in the Commons were harsher. 'For the economic bullies of Supply nights, season after season, a raid at Sir Charles Barry was a sure card for a little cheap popularity at the House of Commons,' commented the *Saturday Review*.

It was scarcely surprising that in 1845 Barry considered resigning. He was no longer able to control or advance the work because his employers – the Office of Woods and Works – had little influence on events, as a minor department of state; as usual the Treasury was questioning every item of expenditure. What they did not question was constantly brought up for scrutiny by Opposition Members in the Commons. The ending of the session each summer, and the annual voting of the estimates, made any programme of expenditure impossible to draw up for more than a few months at a time. At the beginning of 1846 the annual harassment of the architect was resumed by a House of Lords Committee, this time with Lord Somerhill in the Chair. Interrogation did not end for the session until 14 August, two days after the opening of the grouse season. By that time the Lords Committee had made four separate reports on the problems of the architect.

'Last July,' began the Lord Chairman, 'you gave an opinion that the Peers might get into the House of Lords this session, with temporary fittings; are you of that opinion now?'

'Certainly not,' replied Barry, 'because no preparations whatever have been made for temporary fittings, no orders having been given for their preparation.'

'How soon, then?' asked the astonished Lord Somerhill.

'I had hoped,' said Barry, 'to have given the Committee a very satisfactory answer to that question; but under the circumstances in which I am placed, and the interference of Dr Reid with my control and authority in this building, I am not able to mention any definite time.'

Barry went on to say that for many months past Reid's interference had most seriously obstructed the whole progress of the work, on which it had been a continued drag. For example, Dr Reid desired the wall at the north end of the House of Lords to be built with openings first of 200 square feet, then of 250 square feet in area; six months later he changed this to 300 square feet. No sooner had work according to those measurements begun than Dr Reid had doubts; four months later the work was suspended at his request because he wished to reconsider the whole scheme of ventilating the debating chamber. Repeated applications, both in letters and interviews, to him to make up his mind had no success. Meanwhile Reid asked Barry to insert an iron floor above the ceiling of the House, and then changed his mind and demanded a wooden floor. At the same time he proposed seven different ways of constructing the flues and chambers in the roof of the House, but he was still vacillating on which was the best and had, so far, failed to reach any firm decision. Again Reid asked that the main smoke flue, which was to receive the smoke from the great open fires throughout the building, should be built immediately above the ceiling, and that the main air intake should be placed above the smoke flue. That work was duly undertaken, but later Dr Reid decided against the arrangement, and required the smoke flue to be transposed above the air intake. For five months Barry had heard nothing further from Dr Reid, either on the ceiling problem or on any other of the many points at issue.

Then there was the floor. At first the floor of the House of Lords was to be entirely perforated, with an enormous dust-bin of iron under the whole of it. Then the dust-bin was to be of some elastic material, such as canvas or oiled silk, the method of securing it being left undecided. Next, not all floor plates were to be perforated, but some left plain, a proposition which was twice altered.

Dr Reid's attention had by this time turned away from floor and ceiling to walls. They should, in his own phrase, be breathing walls. Air should issue from a bench or seat at each end of the House, in conjunction with air fountains in the form of tables. For the ingress of air alone, eight different proposals had been enunciated by the good doctor, but no drawings, descriptions or practical instructions had been issued for any of them.

With much more evidence of this kind before them, it is almost unbelievable, except to those familiar with the working of Parliament, that the Committee were content to recommend that Dr Reid 'should immediately prepare plans, showing the manner in which he proposes to introduce the air into the House', and expressing their confidence that 'the House of Lords may without difficulty be completed with permanent fittings, for the opening of Parliament next year'.

This inept and impossibly optimistic conclusion was reached after Barry had given evidence that 'matters are now in a perfect state of stagnation as to proceeding with the finishings of any portion of the building'. He warned the Committee that the theory on which Reid was basing his ideas for ventilation was not new. The only novelty, 'and a startling one it is', consisted in applying it to such a vast building as the new Palace of Westminster. All the air was to be taken in at one or other end of the great building, according to the direction of the wind, and after passing through every room, drift up and out through Reid's as yet unbuilt central tower, mingling as it went with the smoke discharged through flues from open fires burning in a thousand rooms. To make such a novel system work, said Barry, 'great mechanical skill, a thorough knowledge of the arts of construction, sound judgement and decision, and in fact the methods and habits of a man of business would be required, in all which attainments and qualities of mind, Dr Reid is, in my opinion, most certainly deficient'.

In fact, Barry was summarizing for the Committee his own personal qualities, but they were not yet prepared to listen to his advice about Reid. At this point the Committee, having heard Reid in furious refutation of Barry, decided that a fresh mind would be of assistance to them in deciding between the rival merits of the architect and the ventilator. They therefore called in a distinguished outsider, Goldsworthy Gurney, who like Barry was later knighted for his public work. Gurney did not waste the Committee's time by adjudicating between Barry and Reid; instead he put forward his own plan for ventilation, which so impressed the Committee that, in a second report, they recommended that the Office of Woods and Works should make further experiments before any plan for ventilation of the building was officially accepted.

By June, however, the Lords Committee had been overtaken by Commons action in setting up a fast-working Committee to speed up Barry's and Reid's mutually antipathetic activities in the area of the Lower House. This new Committee established new records in the scale of scrutiny by question and answer. The Lords Committee were not willing to cooperate in any plan which might involve further postponement of work on their House. They re-examined Barry and as a result of his repeated assertions, decided to back him against Reid, recommending that the ventilation of the House of Lords should be on a plan of his own. But this was not conclusive. Reid accused Barry of giving false evidence, and the Lords Select Committee felt bound to give him a chance to elucidate this charge in another long question-and-answer session.

How was it possible for a gathering of learned men to be so fooled by Reid's bombast? The explanation must be that his evidence was, to amateurs, almost as convincing as Barry's and so much more flattering. As a ventilator, he claimed that he was always paying deference to the architect in everything connected with the structure, stability and ornament of the Houses, as well as the convenience of the building. His task would be eased if ventilation were the sole consideration, but, alas, he told the Committee 'you cannot cut and carve as you like'. Moreover the central tower was the key to everything; until that was built, nothing permanent would be arranged. It was a point of principle that Parliament should get quit of the bad surrounding air: 'We must either confine the ventilation or purify that air. In the new Houses one of the great objects was, the atmosphere outside being so bad, to carry away all that vitiated air together, and to remove it to a vast distance.'

His intentions were recalled the following year when, in the summer heat, the stench of untreated sewage in the Thames was so bad that Members were forced to flee from a committee room, overcome by the 'pestilential odours', and Disraeli aptly described the river as 'a Stygian pool, reeking with ineffable and unbearable horrors'.

The good air, Dr Reid now declared, was to be drawn from 'a great height, from the greatest possible altitude'. The Committee was impressed with this breadth of vision. As he explained, 'the great peculiarity of the new building is that the numerous courts would be a receptacle of vitiated air, but by carrying it away in one central tower all the vitiated air will be removed entirely'. The courtyards, of course, were a fundamental part of Barry's design, and were calculated by him to provide all the air and light which would be necessary. Yet once again the confidence engendered by Dr Reid carried the day.

The Commons, although not quite so blindly complacent as in earlier examinations of Barry and Reid, still believed there was virtue in both men working together. In August the Commons Select Committee at least recognized that 'differences existed' between Barry and Reid; in future, while Barry should carry out Reid's plans as submitted, each man should refer any difference which arose to a conference of one nominee appointed by Barry, and one by Reid. If these two 'third parties' could not decide, then an umpire appointed by the First Commissioner of Woods and Works should settle the argument. With that decision, and with a final compliment on the great improvement which Dr Reid's system had effected in the atmosphere of the temporary House of Commons, the Commons Select Committee dispersed with the feeling that its work had been well done, and that no further obstacles to the completion of the new Palace of Westminster could possibly be foreseen.

Unfortunately, as Barry was quick to perceive, recommendations by Select Committees required the approval of the House before they could be acted upon. It is impossible to appreciate the strain under which Barry was working without a picture of the unending inquisition by Select Committees to which he was subjected at every stage of construction.

In 1850 *The Times* commented scathingly: 'A Select Committee of the House of Commons is justly regarded as one of the most searching and formidable engines of inquiry ever invented by man. Its powers of analysis are almost preternatural. No furnace is so hot, no alembic so penetrating, as a dozen gentlemen of long parliamentary practice, empowered "to send for persons, papers and records", to ask what questions they choose, publish what they choose and to pronounce what judgments their own happy instincts and absolute liberty may suggest. Probably there is no man, no hero, no associated phalanx of heroes, that would not tremble to find itself referred "upstairs" to this compendious manual of parliamentary omnipotence. There is nothing within the reach of mortal ken which it cannot bring to light and expose to the gaze of an envious and uncharitable world. We of the nineteenth century witness its maturity. Something between a Parliament and a jury – for no soil could have produced it except that of trial by jury and representative institutions – it holds in one hand the staff of counsel and in the other the sword of execution. Could we imagine a court in which the counsel, judge and jury were all one, and in which, accordingly, all the unscrupulous talents of partisanship, all the gravity of legal exposition and all the responsibility of a verdict were combined in a dozen men, who had won that position by success in the battle of life, we should find that idea very tolerably realized in a Select Committee of the British House of Commons.'

It was not only as a witness before Select Committees that Barry was under strain. There at least he could score in his replies to his interrogators. Now he had to endure criticism by the House of Commons itself, which left no opportunity for any explanation by the architect. In December 1847 the costs and delays of the building began to exasperate the Commons. Sir Robert Inglis MP, who had been sympathetic to Barry when serving on several committees, now inaugurated a debate in the House on a motion urging that a new Select Committee be appointed on the present state of the building, 'with a view to the reception and accommodation of this House therein'.

It was the occasion for a grand attack on Lord John Russell's Whig government, for its lack of control of expenditure, with many sorties against Barry himself. Ralph Bernal Osborne MP declared that 'a more profligate and gross expenditure of public money had never taken place', and while claiming that he was not attacking the architect personally, alleged it was nevertheless 'a gross job'. Barry was asked to lay a paper estimating the cost of the entire work, and he reckoned that on completion this would be £1 400 000. Joseph Hume MP, a perpetual critic of extravagance in public expenditure, declared that 'Mr Barry should be put under curb and bridle, for he has had his own way too long.' Another Member thought that at a time when the revenue was diminishing, Parliament ought to be intent on economy instead of 'founding magnificent palaces of Gothic architecture'. The response of the government was to praise Barry and the Fine Arts Commission and to defend the estimates which the Treasury itself had approved. Sir Robert Peel gave the House an example of responsible opposition when he put the blame not on the government of the day but upon the House itself, first for insisting on limitations of expense and then for expressing dissatisfaction with the poor results obtained after the required limits had been imposed. A government supporter claimed that Select Committees were not the remedy because, he argued, they invariably added to the expense: 'It often happened that the Government was seized with a cold fit of economy; but Committees were more frequently visited by those warm excesses.' After some days of verbal badminton in true parliamentary tradition, the debate turned on whether a Select Committee was in fact the best vehicle. Osborne, the Member who had previously denied any wish to attack the architect, now moved an amendment; after letting fly at both Barry and Reid he proposed a Royal Commission instead of a Select Committee, since the latter would be, in his view, 'the most incompetent body in the world to decide on any matter of taste, or to control the expenditure of money on matters of taste'.

To moderate the invective, and to yield to renewed pressure from the House, the Ministers changed their ground. Yes indeed, said the Chancellor of the Exchequer, a Royal Commission should be appointed. Some four months after the debate began, in April 1848, a Royal Commission was duly set up. Its membership was limited to three, no doubt on the principle that the fewer the participants the more expeditious would be its work. Indeed it has been frivolously held that the ideal committee consists of three persons, of whom one is away ill and another unavoidably absent. In this case nothing had started more propitiously. Earl de Grey from the Lords and Thomas Greene from the Commons sat under the independent chairmanship of Sir John Fox Burgoyne, Inspector General of Fortifications.

First they were to superintend the completion of the new Palace of Westminster with reference to the designs approved and the amount of the estimates laid before Parliament, and secondly to approve the decorations, furniture, fittings, clocks and bells to complete the Palace, and to decide upon all the arrangements for heating, lighting and ventilation. Since the Treasury, in consultation with the Office of Works, remained in overall financial control, the new Royal Commission soon became more like an additional brake than an accelerator of the work. When in February 1849 the architect was required to estimate for them a final sum for completion of all that they required, he must have had a modest satisfaction in producing the figure of a further £1 025 000, in addition to the £1 400000 on which the fierce debate in the Commons had arisen the previous year.

Meanwhile, Barry had once more reminded the government that he awaited an appropriate settlement of his own remuneration as architect for the building, and later that year the government did concede an inadequate £5000 on account, additional to the original sum of £25 000 prescribed eleven years previously. The new payment was, of course, an admission that the original fixed fee had been inadequate, but Barry's argument for the normal architect's remuneration of 5 per cent on the outlay was never conceded.

Not unexpectedly, the Commons returned to the attack when the following session opened in 1850. This time the causes of delay were attributed not only to Barry and the new Royal Commission of three, but to the architectural and decorative activities of the Fine Arts Commission under Prince Albert. It was discovered, for example, that Landseer had been paid £1000 for three pictures to hang in the Lords' refreshment room, and the Commons on a division of 94 votes to 75 reduced the estimate by that amount. Joseph Hume suggested another Select Committee was now the answer, but once again Sir Robert Peel used his authority on the opposition benches to defeat this move. By this time, however, the Commons' new Chamber was at last ready and Members moved in for a trial sitting. Sir Benjamin Hall, whose virtue was claimed to be that 'he could shut his ears to the blandishments of Mr Barry', presided over yet another Select Committee of the House, which recommended a lower ceiling. 'Any schoolboy would be flogged for designing such a place,' observed Joseph Hume, in the same breath declaring that the change now proposed would destroy the appearance of the chamber.

All this controversy proved too much for the new Royal Commission of three. Next year, in a classic statement of the difficulties which to this day hinder the service of Parliament, they expressed their 'strong impression that it is desirable to put an end, as early as convenient, to an organization that leads in some degree to a mixture of duties and responsibilities by two independent bodies in the management of one concern'. The Royal Commission then volunteered its own dismissal, and in 1851 was dissolved by Royal Warrant, leaving only the authorities of each House, the Lords and Members and a plethora of new Committees to battle on against the government and the Office of Works, with the Treasury and the Fine Arts Commission intervening as before.

It has sometimes been assumed that, compared with the present economic confusion, the Victorians knew what they were doing. In fact, the ship of state was rocking as violently then as now. The changes of government and of policy, with alternating desires for expenditure and for economy, made the construction of the new Palace not only slower but eventually far more expensive than it would have been if the architect had been given consistent support at each stage. Even the government department to which he was answerable changed its form and title as time went on. The Office of Works and the architects it employed had been under parliamentary scrutiny for some time, particularly over extravagance at Buckingham Palace. When Barry began his work, the Office had for several years been combined for the sake of economy with the Office of Woods and Forests, with the Office of Land Revenues being thrown in for good measure. From 1851, however, Woods and Works, as it was usually called, split up again and the Office – or, later, Ministry – of Works continued on its inconspicuous way until in 1970 it became swallowed up in the top-heavy conglomerate known as the Department of the Environment. So Barry started under Woods and Works, with a Whig government under the engaging and genial Prime Minister, Lord Melbourne, whom Grenville described in his diary as 'too fastidious to be a good party man'. When a peer canvassed for a further honour, Melbourne asked in a tone of distaste, 'What does he want now – is it a garter for the other leg?'

Since Parliament is not only supreme but supremely critical, its internal affairs have always been the particular concern of the head of government, for it is from Parliament that the head of government must emerge and Parliament alone can unmake him if it so chooses. Consequently, even the most trivial activities affecting the internal problems of each House tend to be given exceptional treatment. The reluctance of successive governments, both Whig and Tory, to intervene with any firm directions over the building of the new Palace is accounted for by an underlying fear of the institution's power. The Minister charged with responsibility for the Office of Woods and Works by the gracious if indolent Melbourne was Lord Duncannon (later Earl of Bessborough), authoritative and ostensibly efficient, who believed in devolving responsibility on to the architect without, however, giving him any clear lead. When the elegant Sir Robert Peel, whom Disraeli described as 'the greatest member of Parliament that ever lived', became Prime Minister in 1841, he appointed Lord Lincoln, a keen amateur architect, but inflexible and tactless, to head the department which Peel himself bluntly described as 'the common sewer of all the flotsam and jetsam of the offices'.

It was the start of the hungry forties, renewed income tax, falling revenues and the terrible Irish potato famine and it was not the time for extravagant building plans. Lord Lincoln was described by Greville as priggish and solemn, inelastic and 'more than useless as a Minister'. His ambition was said to be in excess of his powers, but Lincoln was witty enough to suggest to Peel that they try out a new fire escape by getting other Ministers to jump from a great height and risk the consequences. He had one great virtue for Barry: he was the only Minister who gave him constant support.

In 1846, Peel was beaten by the pallid and long-suffering Whig, Lord John Russell who, as Prime Minister, now entrusted the Office of Works to Lord Morpeth (later Earl of Carlisle). The new Minister proceeded to give Barry sole control over ventilation of the House of Lords, and Dr Reid that of the House of Commons, thus prolonging rather than resolving the disputes between the two men. Lord Derby, a Tory, and Lord Aberdeen, a Peelite, followed each other as Prime Minister. Barry's last notable mentor was another Whig, Lord Seymour, who as Minister in charge of the Office of Works, thirsted for economy at all levels and down to the smallest detail. In the weekly estimates for the Houses of Parliament, he noticed an item for the employment of a carpenter under Dr Reid and asked what the carpenter was doing and how soon his employment would cease to be necessary. Fresh from his challenge on the £14 cost of a thousand cast-iron labels for naming the plants at Kew Gardens, the diligent Minister complained that two clerks of the works at the new Palace of Westminster were paid as measurers, and that was Barry's responsibility. It was a popular line, since Members of both Houses claimed that the expenditure on the new Parliament was by 1850 altogether out of hand. Joseph Hume, still the most constant critic of expenditure in the Commons, said he did not wish to see any more public buildings unless there was a responsible person in charge to guard against any increase in cost. Another Member (O'Brien Stafford) declared, 'If the blame was charged on Mr Barry, he charged it upon a Committee, the Committee charged it upon another Committee, both the Committees put it upon the Woods and Works, the Woods and Works charged it on the Government and the Government upon the House.'

It must not be thought that Barry's controllers were only the Ministers and government of the day, alternating as they did every three or four years throughout his work of construction. He had more permanent supervisors in the authorities of each House such as the Lord Great Chamberlain, who held hereditary office, and the Speaker of the House of Commons, Charles Shaw-Lefevre, whose tenure of office ran from 1839 to 1857. Apart from his membership of the Fine Arts Commission, where no doubt his influence contributed to some of the ornate decorations of the Speaker's House, the Speaker had often to communicate the needs and complaints of the Commons to the architect. The Speaker's house itself occupied a splendid site facing the river and comprised some 60 rooms in the new building. A young South American visitor to the Houses of Parliament, informed of this fact during a later occupancy, observed with a worldly sigh, 'Ah yes, I suppose they are full of beautiful girls.'

When the Speaker came to retire, he felt that his own work for the House in all fields of responsibility was receiving scant recognition from the government. Its proposal to confer a barony on him, with the Grand Cross of the Bath order, was clearly not good enough. The Clerk Assistant, Erskine May, who had a gifted pen, was required to express on paper his personal view of all that the Speaker had done for the House of Commons. A sycophant of real ability, as his subsequent career was to prove, Erskine May devoted himself to this task with so much enthusiasm that Palmerston, as Prime Minister, the day after getting the memorandum, informed the Speaker that he would be created a Viscount, an honour which as Viscount Eversley he lived to enjoy till 1888 when he was 95. Apart from his service in the House and subsequent longevity, Speaker Shaw-Lefevre had other claims to the attention of historians. Through his marriage into the brewing family of Whitbread, dray horses from the brewery were used to drag on ceremonial occasions the Speaker's brake-less state coach, weighing 2¾ tons, an onerous honour which Whitbreads have maintained to this day. He was also the last Speaker to be allowed to take away the splendid silver dinner service which was provided by the government for banquets in the Speaker's house. It was Joseph Hume MP who pointed out that the Speaker's tax-free salary of £5000 a year should not require to be supplemented by such extras; and after Shaw-Lefevre there were no gifts, only a pension.

CHAPTER SIX

CLOCKS AND
BELLS

1847

The exit of Dr Reid in 1846 was by no means the end of the confusion caused by appointing experts without reference to the architect. The clock tower in Barry's plan, standing above the Commons at the north end of the building, had been in progress since 1843. The internal shaft, measuring 11 feet by 8 feet 6 inches, seemed ample to contain any clock which was likely to be required, and the architectural arrangements went forward. It was not until the tower had reached 150 feet that it was decided by the Office of Works to get plans and specifications for the clock. A Pall Mall clockmaker named Vulliamy was asked to prepare a design for a fee of 200 guineas, to be reduced to 100 guineas if he should subsequently be employed to make the clock. Vulliamy agreed to these terms in April 1844. Fifteen years were to pass before the sound of the striking clock was heard, and within two months the great bell was found to be cracked. It was not until 1862, two years after Barry's death, that the damage was repaired and the famous clock with its great bell finally installed as it is today. Another long story of disappointment and anxiety lay between the start and finish of a vehemently controversial operation, marked once again by governmental ineptitude, professional jealousies and attacks on Barry.

Two years after Mr Vulliamy had been commissioned to design the clock, the government was persuaded that, owing to the importance of the project, there should be a closed competition for the work under conditions laid down by the Astronomer Royal, Professor George Airy, and the plans submitted to him as arbitrator. The clockmakers named as competitors in addition to Vulliamy were Whitehurst of Derby and E. T. Dent of London. Vulliamy completed his drawings and sent them in with a refusal to enter into any competition arranged by the Astronomer Royal. The reason seemed clear enough, for the Astronomer Royal was already committed to E. T. Dent, to whom he had written that if consulted by the government he would unhesitatingly recommend him as the clockmaker, since Dent's clock at the Royal Exchange was, in his opinion, 'the best in the world'.

Not surprisingly, when in 1847 the two surviving competitors submitted their drawings and specifications for the work, the Astronomer Royal reported that Dent was the winner, although to be fair his tender was considerably lower than Whitehurst's. Next year there was a new development. A fierce letter to Lord Morpeth from a Mr E. B. B. Denison QC alleged that Barry was acting in concert with Vulliamy to set aside the decision of the Astronomer Royal and to prevent Dent getting the order for the clock. It seems unlikely that Barry was taking any partisan attitude or had any special interest beyond his desire to get the work finished.

Vulliamy now applied for his promised 200 guineas, perhaps in the hope that the pinchpenny authorities would, even at this late stage, think it cheaper to award him only 100 guineas together with the contract to make the actual clock. His attempt failed, however, if that was indeed his motive. Although it was now 1849 and another year had slipped by, the Commissioners for the New Palace refused to recommend a payment of more than 100 guineas, on the ground that no decision had yet been taken on who would make the clock. Two years later, towards the end of 1851, Lord Seymour, as the responsible Minister at the Office of Works, decided that Denison was the right man to take charge. The clock was to be made by Dent to Denison's own specification for £1800 within two years, after the Office of Works had endorsed his decision that none of the earlier plans would do. Professor Airy and Denison were to be in joint control of the operation and it was not long before a ferocious controversy with Barry was under way.

In a letter to *The Times*, Denison referred to 'his crew of hand-makers and certificate-writers' and accused him and them of stupidity. Professor Airy felt compelled to resign in order to dissociate himself from this sort of unrestrained abuse. About this time, Dent, the winning clockmaker, died, and his son, after some more official wrangling, succeeded to the contract and by 1855 had actually made the clock. This marked the opening of a new offensive which was to last another four years.

St Stephen's Tower had now been built, and after waiting in vain for some information about the bells, Barry roofed in the Tower in 1856. A year earlier he had told the Office of Works that the roof was ready to be erected, but there was no sign of the bells being ready as the tenders for them had only just been accepted. It is not usual when building a church tower to await the casting of its bells, although whenever practicable it is obviously easier to hang bells from above before the tower has been roofed in. But the architect had nothing to do with the clock and bells, although he recommended Denison, as supervisor of the clock, to supervise the bells as well. This was generous of Barry in view of the abuse he had already suffered from the excitable Denison; or perhaps he already foresaw the fiasco which was threatened and had no wish to see Denison evading a contentious issue. At any rate, the clock was finished and the younger Dent was paid £1600 on account – £200 short of the full sum contracted for. This was perhaps prudent, though not generous. It was not Dent's fault that the clock could not be hoisted to its place below the roof of St Stephen's Tower.

As a piece of workmanship, the clock was first class and reflected great credit on both Dent and the irascible Denison. The latter was now ready for a new round of attack and, once more, used *The Times* as battlefield. The question on which the renewed jousting took place was whether the clock was waiting for the Tower or the Tower waiting for the clock. It was a futile argument since neither proposition could stand examination. The clock was ready in 1855 and the Tower, after a year's vain wait for the bells, was roofed in 1856. It was the bells and not the architect that were the cause of the delay, and the bells could not be cast until the tenders for the work were accepted by the government. Of the bell foundries known to

him, Barry recommended four, with a special commendation for
Mears of Whitechapel.

Before the clock could be hoisted, the bells had to be placed above
it, one big hour bell and four smaller bells for striking the quarter
hours. The bells had still to be made. The First Commissioner of
Works was to be an official referee of the casting process. Denison
immediately took strong exception to this, on the ground that the
Commissioner would be technically unversed and therefore likely
to act on the advice of what Denison described as 'somebody behind
the scenes'. A delay accordingly occurred until a new Commissioner
of Works, Sir Benjamin Hall, took control and gave over responsibility for superintending the casting of the great bell to Denison
and two colleagues.

The first Big Ben (called, it is said, after the Commissioner, or,
less probably, after a contemporary seventeen-stone pugilist, Benjamin Caunt) was cast by Messrs Warner in their bell-foundry at
Stockton-on-Tees. This was the hour bell. The four quarter bells
were cast by the same firm at their London foundry in Cripplegate.
Big Ben was brought to Westminster by sea in August 1856. It
required a clapper of unusual weight, and while being tested in the
courtyard of the new Palace before being hung, the bell developed
a crack four feet long, and in October 1857 was removed for re-
casting. This time the work was entrusted to the firm whom Barry
had specially recommended, Mears of Whitechapel. By the following
autumn the great bell was ready again and, this time, with difficulty
hoisted up St Stephen's Tower. In July 1859 Big Ben began to
strike the hours until September, when it was found to be cracked.

Recriminations, charges and counter-charges led this time to an
action in the High Court brought by Mears against Denison, the
intemperate superintendent of their work. The abuse of Barry was
a continuing by-product of the dispute. Denison told a commission
of inquiry that all architects were ignorant of ventilation and that
the ceilings of both Houses were in such a state that 'they might be
set on fire at any instant' following ventilation work reported to
have cost £200000. This was a gratuitous aside which was later
rebutted by Barry's son when he pointed out that the only combustible materials in the roof of the Commons were the fittings placed

there by the experts in ventilation and lighting – Dr Reid and his successors.

Meanwhile up in the Tower, the hour had to be struck on one of the quarter bells. Re-entering the controversy, the Astronomer Royal recommended that a lighter hammer should strike the hours on the great bell and that it should be turned to provide an uncracked surface to the clapper. At last his solution was found acceptable and from 1862 Big Ben rang out the hours while the clock ticked away below.

By this date, however, there was no opportunity for Charles Barry, who had been so abused for his minimal role in the affair, to receive any praise for the successful installation.

While recriminations over the Clock Tower and its bells were seething at the north end of the new Palace, Barry was devoting himself to the immense task of raising the tallest tower in Britain at the south end. The King's Tower, as originally designed, was to be a kind of foursquare castle keep; it was now being changed into the soaring Victoria Tower, named in honour of the Queen. Barry knew the problems and dangers of what he was aiming to erect. He was well aware of James Wyatt's disastrous design for Fonthill Abbey, built in Wiltshire as a gigantic folly for the eccentric millionaire, William Beckford. Its tower was 276 feet high, but the solid foundations underneath had never, through neglect by the busy architect and deliberate deceit on the part of the builders, been laid. The fact was revealed on his deathbed by a repentant Clerk of the Works; Beckford, astute as well as romantic in his ideas, is said to have sold out a few years after its completion and before the stormy night when the whole wonderful tower disintegrated.

Excavations for the Victoria Tower revealed quicksands and springs, yet Barry made no mistakes over the foundations for the Tower, which was to be at least fifty feet higher than Wyatt's at Fonthill. He moved cautiously in ordering only thirty feet of its wall to be constructed every six months. Yet he must already have had anxieties over the soft stone he was using in its construction. The deleterious effect of London's atmosphere, due to sulphur oxides in the air, was already becoming apparent. Granite, with which he had faced the river wall, would have survived, but it was virtually incapable of being carved with any intricate design.

He knew that the secret of architecture lay in proportion, and the mighty garland of Tudor roses and crowns in stone flung all round the vast pointed arches would not conceal any basic fault in design. From the time that he had studied Giotto's fourteenth-century *campanile* of the cathedral in Florence, Barry was aware of the difficulty of designing a tower without it appearing to taper when viewed from below. To avoid this effect of diminution, the design and arrangement of the greater and smaller windows, the niches, cornices, domed turrets and high roof gave him immense trouble. Inevitably, too, official directions he had received for division of floors were countermanded after the work had begun, and altered again at a later stage when rooms in the Tower were to be arranged as a muniment store to be shared by both Houses.

More and more of his time was taken up with what he came to regard as his finest work, by which he hoped to be remembered. There was a special problem in raising the height while retaining the original idea of an entrance under the square keep through which the royal coach was to drive for the opening of Parliament by the Queen. Steel was not yet in use, and Barry had to create a fifty-foot high opening, and then, over the apex of the great arch above the Sovereign's entrance, to construct eight stone floors as well as a top hamper weighing 726 tons. It was a daunting prospect for any architect.

His solution was to use what was then a new building material and support the whole upper part of the tower on eight cast-iron columns, between eight and fourteen inches in diameter. Instead, however, of being embedded in the foundations, the columns rested on four large girders held in their turn by iron templates fixed to the walls above the royal entrance. As a building material, cast-iron was expensive and in a fire it would melt and lose its strength. Barry must have held his breath when Queen Victoria first drove in under the great arch in 1852. Shortly afterwards, probably on the prompting of Prince Albert rather than the usual official channels, she knighted the architect. It was not until a hundred years had passed that a major and hasty rescue operation was found necessary to save the Victoria Tower from the threat of imminent collapse.

CHAPTER SEVEN

A SHAMEFUL
ACCUSATION

1860

Charles Barry's success, his overweening self-confidence in his work and his ability to get his own way in most matters affecting the new Palace continued to inflame his professional enemies. They could not now pull down the building, against which they had vainly petitioned Parliament, but they might be able to pull down the architect himself. The unwitting instrument of this exercise was not hard to find. It was Augustus Welby Pugin, Barry's eccentric collaborator in the months during which he was striving to win the competition. Pugin himself was innocent of any malice, but his lightest aside was noted and stored for reference. Was he not heard to say, when the Office of Works appointed him to be head of wood carving for the new building, 'Barry shall not now have all the credit'?

Young Pugin's fame began in 1835, when he became a convert to Catholicism. He was an impassioned publicist for the faith, but his intense love for the decorative arts suggests the attractions of the church were perhaps as much outward as spiritual. Officiating as an acolyte at a service in Salisbury soon after his conversion, he wrote, 'Our dresses which are handsome and quite correct were worked by the ladies of the chapel and I assure you you would hardly know me when issuing from the sacristy door in full canonicals.'

He was an outstanding writer on his chosen theme. Cardinal Newman did not exaggerate his brilliance when he declared, 'Catholics owe him a great debt for what he has done in the revival of Gothic architecture among us. . . . But he is intolerant and if I might use a stronger word, a bigot. The canons of Gothic architecture are to him points of faith, and everyone is a heretic who would venture to question them.'

Although Pugin was not the originator of the Gothic revival in Victorian England, he gave the necessary inspiration to Gilbert Scott and many later imitators to cover the land with the now familiar spires and mullioned windows of a thousand carbon copies. Gothic churches and houses, Gothic banks and even Gothic barns have left their mark in every part of the country, becoming more typical of Britain than the Saxon towers of older times.

'I was awakened from my slumber,' wrote Scott, 'by the thundering of Pugin's writings.' It was extraordinary that so erratic a man was able to work in harmony with the strong-minded Barry. Sir John Betjeman has pointed out the complete contrast between the two architects: 'Pugin was a medievalist, a devoted Roman Catholic, and presumably an old-fashioned Tory. Barry was a Liberal and a strong Protestant. As so often happens with opposites these two men got on well together.'

Rumours began as early as 1845 that Barry was not the originator of the winning design for the new Parliament, but that it had been done for him by Pugin. It was generally accepted that Pugin made drawings of detail for Barry in 1835, but the larger claim that the winning designs for the whole building were also Pugin's was now whispered.

Before he was twenty, young Pugin had designed furniture for Windsor Castle and stage sets for the theatre. In today's terms he would have been denigrated as arty, crafty and over-fond of dressing up as a common sailor. For he loved sailing and was no great success as a family man, in spite of, or perhaps because of three marriages and the almost inevitable Victorian brood of eight children. 'There is nothing worth living for,' he claimed, 'but Christian architecture and a boat.'

Pugin was the son of a Frenchman who had come to London in 1792 and worked as a draughtsman in the office of John Nash, later famous as the designer of Regent Street. He learned from his father the complexities of Gothic ornaments and assisted him in editing

books on Gothic architecture. Soon his own brilliance as a draughtsman brought tangible rewards. Barry was the first to recognize the
genius which underlay his eccentricities, and let him have full rein,
particularly in his interior decoration of the new Palace of Westminster.

The Chamber of the House of Lords showed what Pugin could
do in the field of ornamentation, and the final design of the Clock
Tower, with the overhanging clock stage extending beyond the
vertical line, is also attributable to Pugin's architectural dexterity.
On the other hand, the most notable of his many churches, St
Augustine's at Ramsgate, was held by Pugin himself to be his own
unaided masterpiece, and must be assessed in the light of that claim.
It is a solid but disappointing structure, without any of the inspiration, either externally or in its interior, that Pugin showed when
devising the great schemes which Barry directed.

Pugin summed up their relationship in his own words, 'I could
not have made the plan, it was Barry's own. He was good at such
work – excellent; the various requirements conveyed by the plan,
and above all the Fine Arts Commission, would have been too much
for me.' Even without those impositions, the pressures of life became too much for him. His designs were used in every part of the
building, both inside and out, and time was also spent in designing
chairs, ink-pots and umbrella-stands. Yet without Barry's master plan,
there would have been a very different result. The pace which Pugin
set himself did in fact kill him nearly a decade earlier than Barry.
Even when he was working on the designs for the competition in
1835 he suffered a few days of temporary blindness, and his eyes
gave him intermittent trouble throughout his working life. His
death at forty, after months of pain and mental illness, followed a
medical diagnosis of 'mania', and in his last weeks before a final
seizure he was sedated with chloroform. Today his malady would
probably be identified as a brain tumour, explaining his frantic
bursts of work and his hallucinations.

Early in 1852 Mrs Pugin learned that an official pension was to be
paid to the already fatally afflicted Pugin. Sir Charles Barry (as he
had just become) was asked to act as trustee. He called on Mrs Pugin
in Hammersmith with various pretexts in order to beg not to be

drawn in. Mrs Pugin was out, but a family friend, the Rev. J. M. Glennie, saw him and years later recalled his extraordinary refusal to help: 'My impression of the interview was one of great disgust, both at the want of feeling shown and the reserved and politic way in which he seemed to be acting; and accordingly I advised Mrs Pugin, whatever she might do, on no account to communicate with him as a friend, and I believe she never did so.' He seemed, as Edward Pugin, her son, wrote, 'studiously desirous to sever, at once, all connection with us, and by ignoring my father's past services, he strove to remove even the faintest suspicion of their real nature'.

Certainly, Barry did not offer sympathy or help on Pugin's death, and failed to subscribe to a proposed memorial. For eight years he made no inquiries about the family, and refused to offer a helping hand to Pugin's eldest son, Edward, then under eighteen, who was striving to cope with the untidy remnants of his father's architectural business.

During the last year of his life, Augustus Welby Pugin was subject to fits of violence and was forcibly restrained from doing himself or his children an injury. Resort to the strait waistcoat must have been a terrible humiliation for his family in an age when mental illness was a shameful secret. At first they maintained him in a private asylum, but later had him moved to Bedlam, the notorious public institution, which could be entered without expense. All this could explain Edward Pugin's bitterness and perhaps also Barry's indifference. Barry's knighthood had added personal dignity but had not silenced the critics. It would be embarrassing to recall how much of his help had come from a man who died insane.

At last, Edward Pugin's indignation drove him to seek a vital interview with Sir Charles Barry on 3 February 1860, during which he produced a series of letters which he claimed would tell their own story: that Barry was helpless without the constant inspiration of the man he called his 'comet' – Augustus Welby Pugin – and who was indeed the real architect of the new building. Edward Pugin claims that on hearing of these letters, Barry asked to be lent them, but later failed to return them. Indeed, if they ever existed, they disappeared and were never recovered. It is understandable that the shock to Barry at the accusation made by the son of his old friend must have been great, but whether or not there was any truth in the accusation, it is a fact that Barry himself died of a heart attack within three months of the interview. It could have been a coincidence, or it could have been despair that after his long struggles for the fame and recognition which he was at last enjoying, the old and relatively innocent deception which had won him the prize was to be brought into the open to destroy him, to delight his enemies and to confirm the suspicions which they had long harboured.

Seven more years passed until, in 1867, Edward Pugin determined to bring to light Barry's total indebtedness to his father by publishing a searing indictment of Barry's pretensions in a polemic entitled 'Who was the art architect of the Houses of Parliament?' Strong arguments have been advanced ever since that date both in support and in rebuttal of Edward Pugin's claims.

The attack is weak on some counts, but the defence of their father's memory by Barry's sons, Charles and Edward, the architects and the Rev. Alfred Barry, his biographer, is also not impenetrable. Edward Pugin, for example, claimed that Barry had paid 400 guineas for the beautifully drawn set of plans which won him the great competition against ninety-six rivals. Stubs of Barry's cheque books revealed that over a four-month period Pugin had been paid almost exactly that sum, i.e. £413 14s. 0d. Against the last payment there are the significant words 'in full'.

The whole history of Barry's own work on the new building is marked by lengthy alterations and hesitations, as the architect drew and redrew his designs. His son, Edward, sought to refute Edward Pugin's allegations by quoting from hundreds of entries to prove the time and infinite study which Sir Charles gave to every detail of his work. Entries relating to the Clock Tower and Victoria Tower are as follows:

1852
22 October Studies of Clock Tower for models.
1853
7 February Details of Victoria and Clock Towers.
30 April Working drawings of Clock Tower. Gave orders for model.

22 August Details of design for Clock Tower. Instructing Mabey as to model.
10 September Modifications of design for Clock Tower. Giving orders for model.
16 September Giving orders for modifying design for Clock Tower.
1854
7 January Working drawings of Clock Tower.
11 April Sketches for roof of Clock Tower.
1855
5 February Making drawing for varying top of Clock Tower.
26 September On design for dormers of Clock Tower.
27 September On design for dial of Clock Tower.
27 November On design for top of Victoria Tower.

After three such years nothing was yet in final form. No wonder young Edward Barry wrote: 'at no time during the years that elapsed between Mr Pugin's death and the completion of the Tower could I have confidently predicted the appearance it would ultimately assume'. His father was, at least in his later years, a fastidious ditherer, requiring to look at ten ways of doing the same thing before reaching a conclusion. The unintended result of this analysis must be to raise doubts on Barry's original competition-winning entry. He had only a few months in which to prepare this entry; the site plan was only put on sale at the Office of Works at the end of July 1835, yet his winning entry, containing drawings of elaborate detail, showing elevations and sections from every angle, was rushed in on the closing date – 1 December 1835. Pugin's diary shows he was working with Barry on plans for the river front and receiving payments from him during the short intervening period.

Charles Barry's close friend and admirer, J. L. Wolfe, gives a different picture. Certainly, he agrees that Pugin worked for Barry on details of the great man's designs. Pugin's drawings were 'rather rough but masterly sketches in pencil . . . dashed in with a facility of a scene-painter'. The sketch of the river front, perhaps the most celebrated of all views of the Houses of Parliament and one which must have clinched Barry's victory in the competition, was produced, according to Wolfe, in this way: to keep his drawings secret, Barry had converted his nursery into a private drawing office, to which nobody was admitted except the faithful Mrs Barry, the devoted Wolfe and a servant. One night when Wolfe was staying in the house, Barry had been talking over the problem with him, and not feeling satisfied had retired to bed in a restless state of doubt. But Wolfe had not been asleep long, when Barry burst into his room exclaiming, 'Eureka! I have got it at last!' and then and there, by the glimmer of a rushlight, rapidly sketched out the grand idea that had 'just struck him. After a short sleep he was at his drawing board, and when I rejoined him, there was the River Front.'

Every aspect of the controversy has elements of doubt and Wolfe's romantic picture, intended to defend his friend's memory, would have been more applicable as an illustration of the impulses and imagination of Pugin than to the meticulous and painstaking Barry.

The Barry family deplored Edward Pugin's attack on the ground that he not only attacked their father's reputation after his death, but also that he dishonoured his own father's memory by suggesting that he was in league with Barry over a fraudulent entry for the competition. There may, however, be a more human explanation of this reckless raking over the bones of the past. Edward Pugin had seen the immense extent of his father's work on the new Palace of Westminster. He knew that without his father's efforts Barry could never have accomplished the great task that faced him. He remembered the cry of despair when after criticism in Parliament Barry wrote from his Brighton sick bed in September 1844:

Dear Pugin,

I am in a regular fix respecting the working drawings for the fittings and decorations of the House of Lords, which it is of vital importance to me should be finished with the utmost possible despatch. . . . I know of no one who can render me such valuable and efficient assistance, or can so thoroughly relieve me of my present troubles of mind in respect of these said drawings as yourself.

And now that my father is dead, Edward Pugin told himself, there is to be no recognition and no adequate reward from Sir Charles Barry for my mother or the eight children which my poor demented father left without support.

(*Top left*) Sir Charles Barry (1795–1860) the architect whose plans won the competition for the new Houses of Parliament. He was an ingenious draughtsman and a bold innovator, but he suffered from criticism and official interference in his progress, the denial of customary fees and allegations against his professional integrity.

(*Top right*) Augustus Welby Pugin (1812–52) a leading church architect in his own right, and Barry's devoted assistant and, later, collaborator. Pugin was a decorative draughtsman and an interior designer as well as being a controversial writer on Gothic and Catholic themes.

(*Bottom*) The old Houses of Parliament before the great fire of 1834. Westminster Hall is shown in the centre with the twin towers of the Abbey on the right. The buildings clustered round the Hall were mainly wooden, and, when the fire swept them away, Barry had to retain the Hall within a coherent neo-Gothic setting.

(*Opposite*) Westminster Hall. Sir Charles Barry made bold additions to the ancient hall, enlisting its hammer beam roof to frame his own design of St Stephen's Porch, reached by wide steps and leading through a great arch.

(*Above*) The Houses of Parliament – the landward side. Barry's impressive façade from St Stephen's Entrance to the Victoria Tower was incomplete without the northern section to enclose New Palace Yard, which he planned but which was never authorized, leaving in his own words 'an irregular, disjointed and incongruous building' facing Parliament Square.

Edward M. Barry (1830–1880) son of Sir Charles Barry. After his father's death in 1860, he was appointed architect for the Houses of Parliament. In 1870, he was abruptly dismissed from his post by a letter which, as a sympathetic Member said, 'no gentleman would send to a butler who had been 30 years in his employment'.

The Fine Arts Commission. A meeting in 1846 to choose works of art for the new Houses of Parliament. Charles Barry, who was not invited to join the Commission, stands answering questions by the Prince Consort, seated below Queen Victoria's bust.

NORTH FRONT OF THE SPEAKERS RESIDENCE AND FRONT TOWARDS NEW PALACE YARD

(*Top*) The Crypt Chapel under St Stephen's Hall. One of the most ancient sites within the royal Palace of Westminster, painstakingly restored by Edward Barry.

(*Bottom*) The new Houses of Parliament from the north. Barry's winning design of 1835. The original plan for a heavy square tower was continuously revised over the years until it emerged as the present Clock Tower.

House of Commons Chamber
1852–1941. With a false ceiling
and windows arbitrarily reduced
in height, Sir Charles Barry
thought the debating chamber
was ill-proportioned and
unworthy of its purpose.

St Stephen's Hall.
The original Commons
debating chamber was
demolished after the great fire
of 1834, and reconstructed as
St Stephen's Hall, an
antechamber leading to the
Central Lobby. The Fine Arts
Commission decided, against
Barry's wish, to encumber it
with marble statues of statesmen
making rhetorical gestures.

(*Top*) Members on the Terrace. The attractions of the Terrace on summer nights could not be enjoyed until after 1865 when the Metropolitan Board of Works, with its chief engineer Sir Joseph Bazalgette, achieved one of the major engineering feats of the century by building 82 miles of sewers instead of polluting the river with sewage. Since ladies had no votes, their presence was exclusively social.

(*Bottom*) The new Houses of Parliament from the river. The foundation stone was laid in 1840. There were many alterations in design before the work was completed in 1870, ten years after Sir Charles's death.

On the other hand, those who spoke for Barry all paid generous tribute to Pugin. They admitted that Barry 'was compelled to get some quick hand to help him' but when it was a question of Pugin acting alone, his success was not so immediate. He had sent in another design in the competition which he drew for the established architect, Gillespie Graham, but it did not secure any recognition by the judges.

Writing later as senior partner of an independent firm, John Clayton, for example, who had worked on the new Palace with both men, expressed the highest admiration for Pugin's genius, but he went on to describe very aptly what is confirmed by the known character of each man: 'The frequent cancellings, modifications and changes wrought upon Pugin's designs by Sir Charles' counselling, sketching and restraining influence generally were often startling to me by the extent to which they were carried.' He and his fellow craftsmen admired with equal enthusiasm 'the force of Mr Pugin's abundant fancy and the power of Sir Charles' artistic judgement'.

The splendidly integrated ground plan, by which there is not so much as a six-inch step between the Queen's Robing Room at one end of the Palace and the distant state rooms of the Speaker a quarter of a mile away, was as obviously Barry's work as was the effect of the steps which lifted Westminster Hall into some sort of conjunction with the other pieces of the new Palace which he had been obliged to fit in between the river wall and the Palace yards. It was his problem not only to design but to build, and in that practical task Pugin played a very minor role.

Yet amid all the conflict of evidence, one episode in Edward Pugin's story has remained mysterious and unexplained. Barry's sons tended to deny that it ever took place. Edward Pugin's memory, however, is explicit and bears the stamp of truth:

From the day of my father's funeral, until Mr Ferrey's *Biography* [of Pugin] was publicly announced, I never, except on one occasion, either saw or heard from Sir Charles Barry. He, who, in one of his latest letters to my father, professed himself to be in 'an agony of suspense' about his life, never troubled himself, for eight years after his death, so much as to enquire after our interests. It was only after I had written to Sir Charles, at Mr Ferrey's request, for the loan of any letters or documents in his possession, bearing on my father's connection with the Parliament Houses, that I found myself once again in his presence. The result of my letter was a visit from him. He assured me that it was impossible to comply with my request, as he had destroyed the whole of the correspondence; and, at the same time, expressed an emphatic hope that all his letters to my father had shared the same fate. I shall never forget his agitation when I informed him that, on the contrary, I was in possession of a vast number of his original letters. His confusion and distress were painful to witness. 'Good Heavens,' he said, 'I thought Pugin destroyed all letters he received.' He was still more agitated, however, when I gave him to understand that I was perfectly aware of the nature of the relations which had all along existed between my father and himself, and that I considered him to be the possessor of honours to which my father had at least an equal right. I further expressed to him my intention of asserting my father's just claims, now that I felt myself in a position to do so; and to obtain for him, as far as lay in my power, a public recognition of his services. In a moment Sir Charles' manner altered. He apparently acquiesced in the justice of my representations; promised that my father's status should no longer remain unacknowledged; guaranteed that every emolument which had been held out to him should, as far as possible, be secured; undertook to look into certain accounts then unsettled; and finally begged me to entrust him with the letters for perusal, on his positive assurance that they should be returned to me.

My step-mother was present during the latter part of the interview, and taxed Sir Charles with his want of consideration in refusing to act as her trustee; hearing with much astonishment, his absolute denial of a fact which took place in his interview with Mr Glennie, and which could never fade from her recollection.

Before leaving the house he received the letters from me, and invited me to dine with him the next evening, when he requested more time for their perusal, and promised to return them by the hand of Lady Barry in a day or two. In the fulfilment of this promise Sir Charles failed; and from that day to this the letters have never been returned. I made several applications for them, which were unnoticed; Sir Charles made evasive excuses when I called upon him for them; paid me another visit, simply to renew these excuses, and, in fine, broke his promise altogether.

To have parted with letters which contained important evidence was, as the event proved, an act of extreme imprudence; but I was inexperienced at the time, and in truth was so thrown off my guard by Sir Charles' graciousness of manner, the apparent interest he evinced for us, and the promises he held out to me, that I would have yielded to almost any proposition he might have made. I forgot, in a moment, that long interval of eight years, during which he had broken off all intercourse with us, and divorced my father's name from his.

Sir Charles Barry's response, which he sent to Mrs Pugin three days after his first visit, bears out much of what Edward Pugin alleged respecting his change of tone and the sudden renewal of his professions of friendship after eight silent years. On 6 February 1860 he wrote from his house at Clapham Common:

Dear Mrs Pugin,

I am much concerned that you should have been under the impression that I could be indifferent to you and all connected with your late husband, whose memory I shall ever cherish and respect, as a warm friend and a man of genius of the highest order. Be assured, my dear Mrs Pugin, that you have been entirely mistaken in supposing that I have ever shown any reluctance to be on friendly terms with you and your family; and that, as to my refusing to become a trustee for your pension, your mention of such a breach of friendship is the first I have heard on the subject. Believe me when I say that I have never heard of any wish that I should take upon myself that office, or I would gladly have responded to it. I am glad, however, of this opportunity to assure you that all your suspicions to my disadvantage are wholly groundless, and, at the same time, to beg of you to believe that I shall always be ready to be of any service in my power to you and yours whenever any opportunity occurs. I have given orders for a statement of the sums paid to Messrs —— in each year consecutively, from the commencement of their employment, and I will take an early opportunity of calling upon you with it, and ascertaining precisely what your farther wishes may be with regard to their connection with your late dear husband in respect of the work supplied,

With kind regards to all your family, believe me,
My dear Mrs Pugin,
Most truly yours,
CHARLES BARRY.

It was difficult to believe his assurances, and up to the time of his death a few weeks later, the Pugin family heard nothing to allay their long-nurtured suspicions.

There is no doubt that Barry owed more to Pugin than he and his family were prepared to acknowledge. Equally, however vital his contribution, Pugin was not the principal architect and never could have accomplished what Barry and his son Edward achieved in that capacity by continuous work over a third of the century, between 1836 and 1870.

There can be no doubt, however, that Barry's memory was effectually tarnished by the public reproaches of the Pugin family.

Naturally Barry's family asked why Edward Pugin had waited so long before launching his accusations seven years after Barry's death. His own explanation was specious but incomplete. He did not have the facts and corroborative evidence at any earlier time, and would have had no chance of obtaining a hearing in the later years of Barry's public fame and recognition. It is probable that what fired the explosion by Edward Pugin was the careful and well-written biography of Sir Charles Barry, published in 1867 by the Rev. Alfred Barry, which barely gives Pugin the importance his great contribution to the work merited. The acknowledgement that he was a very helpful subordinate in charge of wood-carving was technically accurate but at the same time wholly inadequate.

Edward Pugin, in fairness, never claimed the totality of the design for his father. Even he allowed the ground plan to be Barry's but claimed that all the elevations and, above all, all the decorations were the exclusive contributions of his father. In an open letter to the members of the Lords and Commons in November 1867 he wrote: 'I earnestly solicit your aid in obtaining for my father the share of fame due to him as the Art Architect of your Houses of Parliament, which has hitherto been unjustly assigned to another.'

This devastating attack on Sir Charles Barry's memory was made at a time when Edward Barry, the most gifted of his sons, was continuing all the architectural work of completing the new Palace, on the lines supposedly laid down by his late father. Professionally it was not deliberately intended, but probably succeeded, in doing the utmost damage to the now prosperous Barry family.

Edward Pugin's intention was not perhaps to destroy the Barry name, but he was on the road to doing so by conceding a little but persevering with the main charge: 'I never sought to depreciate his manifold labours and persevering efforts on behalf of the "great work"; for well enough I know that he was indefatigable. Sir Charles Barry was no carpet knight. He did not seek the assistance of my father in order that he himself might enjoy immunity from labour, but because he knew that he possessed neither the knowledge nor the feeling of Gothic art. It is no disparagement to the greatness of his undoubted abilities, and the extent of his actual services to define accurately what those services were, and no longer to permit him to usurp the credit of work which another performed.'

Edward Pugin's purpose was to establish that his father should be considered at least the joint architect of the Houses of Parliament. His pamphlet was illustrated with a faded photograph of a design for a great Gothic château drawn by his father in 1833, the year before the Great Fire. His aim was undoubtedly to suggest resemblances to the new Houses of Parliament. Except for the mullioned windows, it did not carry overmuch conviction. It was enough, however, to set the Barry sons alight with indignation and provoke their energetic attempts at refutation. The best the sons could produce was a solitary drawing of what was claimed to be a wholly original Barry design for the highly ornamental interior of the House of Lords. This single example was defaced and dirty, as it had been used for several years at the Thames Bank workshops. There were dozens of Pugin's designs which have survived to this day to demonstrate his skills as a draughtsman and artist, yet the Barry family's keenest researches could produce no more than one drawing by Sir Charles himself. Worse, their challenger descried among the carving on the original drawing of 1841 what looked like the initials A. W. P. The explanation that these initials probably represented a heraldic compliment to the heir to the throne, Albert Prince of Wales, was nullified by the fact that he had not yet been christened.

Modern researchers have not got much beyond the conclusion that all the designs for the new Palace were done under the 'incessant direction' of Barry, and that Pugin's own work was frequently modified on his instructions, to fit in with the overall requirements of the building.

After Pugin's death, there was no relaxation for Barry. In spite of his knighthood and public recognition, the strains of work, anxiety

and disappointment wore him down. There was constant deprecia-
tion of his achievement by parliamentarians. Lord Brougham's
verdict of some years earlier had found increasing support: 'Mr
Barry was not only a Gothic architect, not only was he a dilatory
man, but the very name of delay itself.' Certainly he had still not
put the finishing touches to the Victoria Tower in 1860, although
it had been generally regarded as complete when the Queen drove
under its great arch eight years before. The seventy-three-foot flagstaff to surmount it was still on Barry's drawing board at the beginning of May 1860, a few days before his sixty-fifth birthday.

On Friday 11 May he was at Westminster as usual. On Saturday
he went to the Crystal Palace for most of the day, apparently quite
fit. Between eight and nine o'clock in the evening he was seized
with 'what appeared to be paralysis' and died within two hours.
The Times referred to the great men of science (Robert Stephenson),
literature (Lord Macaulay) and art (Barry) who had all died within
the past few months. The report recalled Barry's main works, King
Edward VI Grammar School in Birmingham, the Travellers and
the Reform Club, the College of Surgeons, and the finest portion
of his Palace of Westminster work – the Victoria Tower. 'As long
as that tower stands, its great founder will need no other memorial
of his fame with posterity.'

An approach by the Institute of British Architects to the Dean of
Westminster obtained permission for Barry to be buried in the
Abbey. The nave was fuller than usual due to 'the number of spectators in bright dresses, as none were admitted near the grave who
were not in mourning'. Viscount Palmerston was the last of the
great men who presided as Prime Minister during Barry's final
years, and who had earlier served on one of the Select Committees
on the new building. On the evening before the funeral, he personally moved the adjournment of the House for a notable event on the
following day – Derby Day. Barry's funeral in the Abbey clashed
with the appointment on Epsom Downs and it was clear which
event would take precedence for the popular Palmerston. His horse
Mainstone was running that day in the Derby and as its owner he
had to be present, although, in the event, it was unplaced.

Barry's life was over but the Commons had not yet finished with him. It was still possible to insult his memory and to harass his son in his filial task of completing the work that remained. Architectural friends thought it appropriate that somewhere in the new Palace of Westminster there should be a monument to its designer. Foley, the sculptor, produced largely from his own memory a fine and effective statue of Barry engaged on his last design – the Victoria Tower. Permission was sought from the authorities to have the statue in St Stephen's porch, marking Barry's successful adaptation of the south end of Westminster Hall as part of the grand entrance to the building, by his addition of the splendid arch, window and staircase. This application was turned down by the Lord Great Chamberlain, but a corner near the foot of the stairway leading up from the Lower Waiting Hall to the Committee floor, virtually out of the sight of visitors, was the best place that could be found for the man who had given so much of his life to the Commons during the years of rebuilding. A subscription for the statue was generously supported by Barry's professional friends and colleagues. The Duke of Newcastle, the most constant of all his official patrons and support-ers, who had warmly endorsed the idea of the statue, gave £20. Sir Morton Peto MP, one of the principal contractors of the Palace, gave twenty guineas and Lord Stanley MP ten guineas. The First Commissioner of Works (Rt Hon. W. F. Cowper MP) gave £10, as did the President of the Institute of British Architects, William Tite FRS, MP. Apart from these four, the only Members of the Commons who contributed were the two Glyns (of the banking family), each of whom gave a guinea. Workmen from Clapham gave £2 14s. 6d. The other Members of the Commons, which at that time numbered 658, gave nothing. Barry would not have been surprised. He had long since realized the extent of the indifference or resentment of that body.

CHAPTER EIGHT

DISMISSED WITHOUT REASON

1870

Years of patient work had at last brought a visible result. There was scarcely a building in England which displayed such a variety of interest when viewed from every possible angle, whether distantly from across the Thames or nearby from the landward side. Even the most bitter of the critics could not now deny the breadth of planning which had lifted the amber stone from the Anston quarries into a new and dramatic skyline to the east of Westminster Abbey. What might have seemed too predictable and austere in the original designs appeared at last as an exciting and calculated asymmetry. Roofs were everywhere visible, but their slopes were concealed behind a screen of gracious pinnacles. Plain façades were now decorated with a fantastic pageantry of kings and queens, heraldic lions, unicorns, crowns and Tudor roses. From every viewpoint the spectator would see a different arrangement of towers and turrets. No two faces of the building looked the same, yet an overall harmony had been achieved. Nevertheless much work still remained when the death of Sir Charles Barry occurred so suddenly.

The Rt Hon. William Cowper MP was First Commissioner of Works and was responsible for making a new appointment to the vacant post of architect. There was no great anxiety in his department to continue the association with the Barry family, but two of Charles Barry's children, Charles the eldest, and Edward the third son, had been successively concerned with the new Palace for so long that there was nobody who could claim to equal either in their special knowledge of the building, quite apart from their high reputation as architects. The eldest brother, Charles, later distinguished enough in his own right to become a President of the Royal Institute of British Architects, had now ceased working on the new building and gone into independent partnership with another of Sir Charles Barry's pupils, R. R. Banks. Together they won second place to Gilbert Scott in the competition for the Foreign Office building in Whitehall. The trouble was that the Barry sons, of whom there were five, were all gifted, and none more so than Edward Middleton Barry. His work on the New Palace was so appreciated by his father that he left him in his will the whole of his drawings and papers relating to the building. With this bequest Edward Barry had been handed the master key of the whole project, and for once the architect, and neither the government nor the Members of either House, had the whip hand. It was a situation which would have gladdened the heart of Sir Charles Barry, and which he would have felt was well merited by his son. After some hesitation Edward Barry was appointed by the Office of Works as his father's successor to continue the work from 1860 as architect of the building. For ten years he carried on, establishing good relations with the parliamentary authorities and gaining increasing approval from committees of each House.

Almost daily, particularly during the session, Edward Barry was called on to produce new designs or to modify existing ones. The magnificent decorations in the Queen's Robing Room, the restoration of St Stephen's Crypt, the completion of the royal staircase and the cloisters leading from the Members' Entrance to the steps below Big Ben are notable examples of his work, which bear comparison with the best in any part of the Palace. There were many others. He gave a new impetus to the work which his father had latterly been so hesitant in finishing. Work on the Clock Tower was now brought to an end. New galleries were built within the Victoria Tower, and the Tower itself, which at the time of Barry's funeral had only a temporary pole to carry a mourning flag at half-mast, was at last completed. Additional mosaics in the Central

Lobby and corridors were laid, the subway to Bridge Street was built, works in New Palace Yard and Parliament Square were carried out, and new stables for the Speaker's coach and horses were constructed at Millbank.

Alterations became necessary inside the Commons, in the Ladies' Gallery and to the roofs of both Houses. Few comments have been made about the ceilings of the halls and chambers on the principal floor of the Palace, but the splendour of the ceilings, particularly in the Queen's Robing Room, are a tribute to the less recognized talent of Edward Barry.

There were so many demands on his time and energy that he had, at his own expense, to set up an office at 21 Abingdon Street in the immediate neighbourhood of the Palace, since there was no accommodation for the architect within the building. As he himself explained, 'from the natural interest I have felt in my father's great work, I have looked on my connection with it with feelings of pride and satisfaction, very different in their nature from those with which an architect regards his ordinary professional engagements'. It is impossible to doubt his sincerity when he said, 'It has been my ardent desire to maintain and supplement my father's work to the best of my ability, and to remove any partial or accidental inconveniences which may obscure those great architectural merits which I may be pardoned for thinking must ever render the New Palace of Westminster the honourable monument of its architect, who devoted to it the best portion of his life.'

Throughout these years Edward Barry received the customary rate of professional fees, namely 5 per cent on outlay, which had been so harshly refused to his father. At the same time he did not exceed his estimates on a single occasion, so Parliament had every reason to be gratified by the appointment.

In 1867 the inconveniences of the cramped Commons Chamber, which Sir Charles Barry had been required to make as small as possible, now led to the setting up of yet another Select Committee to inquire into what could be done to give Members more space. A Minister – Mr Hunt, Secretary of the Treasury – told the Committee that almost every evening, in the busiest part of the session, he was obliged to stand, sometimes for hours, with a crowd of other

Members behind the Speaker's Chair, ready to come forward and squeeze into a seat on the Treasury bench when his turn came to answer a question concerning his department. The validity of his complaint would be recognized by every Commons Minister today.

Edward Barry was called on to assist the Committee in making sketches of various ideas put before them and, indeed, to do more than that. It was resolved 'That Mr Barry be further requested to prepare any plan his good sense may suggest'. It was a remarkable vote of confidence in Barry's judgement and he was soon able to put before the Committee a strikingly original plan. The debating Chamber would be left as a spacious lobby or ante-chamber leading to a large square hall which would constitute a new House of Commons. There would be several additional benefits. The proposed new House would involve using the adjoining courtyard and dining rooms, but the loss of the Commons Court would be more than compensated for by the other improvements. The dining rooms would be moved to terrace level and given more light and air from enlarged windows overlooking the river. The need for Ministers' private rooms could be met by taking over space occupied by the residences of the Assistant Serjeant at Arms and other officers of the House. In Barry's view, there was no need for these residences to be so close to the House; they could easily be moved out towards Bridge Street if Sir Charles Barry's original design to enclose New Palace Yard with a dignified new quadrangle was now carried out. Another benefit of the new plan would be the removal of the unsightly ceiling in the present Chamber and 'the restoration of the apartment to its original handsome architectural character, as designed by my father'.

The Select Committee were clearly impressed with Barry's scheme, but preferred to report it to the House without themselves pronouncing for or against its merits. *The Times* wrote an appreciative leading article saying that the Commons had been gradually acquiring more confidence in itself and that it was now extending that confidence to the House of Commons of the future: 'It is now about to stretch the cords and enlarge the tabernacle.'

Two days later the Editor received a brief but acid letter from Edward Pugin claiming that it was not Sir Charles Barry but

Augustus Welby Pugin who had designed the new Palace of Westminster, and that both the false inner ceiling of the debating chamber and the original one above it were his father's work. He urged readers of *The Times* to await the imminent publication of his pamphlet attacking the pretensions of the Barrys. Apart from the embarrassment caused by these allegations, Edward Barry's confident plans proved distasteful to Gladstone's new government, which displaced that of Disraeli in 1868, and were laid aside.

There were other clouds on the horizon, and soon Edward Barry was to find that surreptitious plans were afoot for his replacement. Concern had been growing for some time over the premature decay of stone; some of the delicate pinnacles and carving on the parapets were in an early stage of decomposition. Fortunately for Edward Barry, the precautions taken by his father in selecting stone made it impossible to blame either architect for this defect in building material. Long before the first stone was laid, Barry senior had suggested to the Commissioners of Woods and Works, in a letter of 5 July 1838, that a group of scientists should tour the country with him to inspect quarries and old buildings in order to select the right type of stone. The government department, having agreed with the proposal, appointed Sir Henry de la Beche of the Geological Survey, Dr William Smith, a geologist and engineer, and Mr Charles Harriott Smith, a master mason who had done stone carving on the National Gallery portico, to accompany Barry and guide his choice. After six weeks and the then considerable sum of £1300 had been spent on the tour, Bolsover stone was chosen and, when the quarries there ran out, Anston stone was substituted. Neither stone proved sufficiently durable to resist the assaults of London rain and smoke.

In 1861, the year after he was appointed, a committee made up of two professors and Edward Barry himself recommended the application of chemical processes to check the deterioration. No immediate action was taken by the Office of Works, but in 1868 Professor Abel made an expert survey of the continuing deterioration; in a critical report to the First Commissioner he expressed the firm view that much of the decay which had occurred since 1861 could have been prevented if the recommendations by Edward Barry and his colleagues had been acted on at the time. Although decomposition had not reached a point when the stability of the whole building was affected, it was natural that whispers should begin about the dangerous state of the new building and the joint responsibilities of the architects, father and son, for what had occurred. By 1869 the decay was getting worse, and Edward Barry wrote to George Russell, the permanent secretary of the Office of Works, urging that the worst stones be removed, and new stones substituted for them. At the same time he reminded the Office that in a building so extensive and elaborate as the New Palace of Westminster, containing so large a quantity of stone exposed to the deleterious influence of London atmosphere, a certain amount of failure in the stone and a consequent need for repairs must be expected. He also pointed out that nothing of this kind had yet been done, although portions of the building had been completed for more than twenty years. The Office of Works were at last thoroughly alarmed. It seemed to them that Barry was trying to avoid blame for the years of neglect. What, they asked, was this all going to cost? Linseed oil, replied Barry, was the answer, but its cost would depend on a most careful examination of the extent to which it might be found necessary to apply the treatment to the stone. It might cost £5000 for the parts most affected; he added, however, that if the recommendations of 1861 had been carried out at that time, the expense would have been less.

The letter containing these warnings of the need for urgent treatment of the stonework went to the Office of Works on 27 May 1869. There was still no action, but it was clear from later events that Barry's warning was worded in too peremptory a tone, all too reminiscent of his father's occasional bluntness when driven to impatience by those he regarded as fools. During the winter of 1869, draft estimates for the work of the coming year were prepared by the Office of Works and as usual submitted to the Treasury for approval, after consultation with the authorities of Parliament on the needs of each House. Edward Barry was now thoroughly disturbed by what seemed to him to have the makings of a disastrous situation. If something were now to occur, such as a fall of stone, he as architect would obviously not escape blame. He felt it imperative to make this position clear in a letter to the responsible Minister.

On 19 January 1870 he therefore described the situation in the plainest terms: 'As I do not hold any appointment in virtue of which the building is in any sense under my charge, and as I have no responsibility in respect of it, except as regards such works as are entrusted to my superintendence from time to time, I feel that I am, perhaps, transgressing the limits of strict official duty in addressing the First Commissioner on this point. I trust, however, that if this is the case, I may be excused in consequence of the great interest I must always feel in this great national building.'

In his letter he warned of the necessity in the coming year to arrest the decay and to preserve the stonework of the Houses of Parliament. 'I am convinced,' he wrote, 'that further delay will greatly aggravate the difficulties and increase the ultimate cost of dealing with the question.' Again he pointed out that much of the decay would have been prevented if his recommendations of 1861 had been acted upon at that time, a view since endorsed by Professor Abel. Finally, he told the Minister (Acton Ayrton) that the smaller pinnacles and other exterior stonework 'may become dangerous if no steps are taken to watch them and secure their safety. I am apprehensive of the consequences of further delay in adopting measures to arrest or prevent the decay of the stone.'

This letter for the Minister was sent off in the normal way to the secretary of the Office of Works, George Russell. Edward Barry did not have long to wait for a reply. Three days later, on 22 January, he got the answer, written by Russell on behalf of the First Commissioner, the Rt Hon. Acton Ayrton.

Ayrton was an ambitious and impatient politician who had been a long time reaching eminence. Born in 1816, he had practised as a solicitor in Bombay. Returning to England, he was called to the bar of the Middle Temple in 1853 and elected a Liberal Member for Tower Hamlets in 1857. Gladstone made him parliamentary secretary to the Treasury at the beginning of his ministry, but within a few months he was promoted to be First Commissioner of Works and made a Privy Councillor in 1869. He did not go much further; after four years he was moved to the post of Judge-Advocate-General for the final year of Gladstone's first administration, but held no later office. His first official letter to Edward Barry was a brief but astonishing document, containing in two sentences only the barest reference to the matters of such great concern to the architect of the New Palace. It was in fact a dismissal notice, written in what seemed a grossly insulting manner:

Sir,

I am directed by the First Commissioner of Her Majesty's Works to inform you that, in consequence of various arrangements now being made for the conduct of works under this office, the new Palace of Westminster will, from the 31st March next, be placed entirely in the charge of the officers of this Department, and that the Estimates for that service for the ensuing year will therefore be prepared on their responsibility.

I am further to inform you that the First Commissioner will be obliged to you to have all the contract plans and drawings of the Houses of Parliament, and all other papers necessary for affording a complete knowledge of the building, and of the works carried on in connection therewith, arranged together, and deposited in the office of the Clerk of the Works, in order that they may, when required, be at once handed over to this Department.

I am &c

GEORGE RUSSELL
Secretary.

Edward Barry was, by any standard, an accomplished architect, who had given many years of his professional life to the service of Parliament. In the previous July he had been made a Royal Academician. It passed his belief that he should be dismissed by a Minister of the Crown in a Liberal government, under William Gladstone as Prime Minister, and with no reason given. It appeared to be an extraordinary action, and he decided it must require an immediate explanation. He therefore wrote a long yet courteous letter to George Russell, submitting a strong case for the Minister's consideration:

As I have hitherto been engaged professionally at the New Palace of Westminster, and as your letter appeared to me to intimate my dismissal from the post I have so long occupied as architect to the building, in order that it might be filled by Captain Galton, the newly appointed Director of Works and Public Buildings, I have communicated with the Chancellor of the Exchequer on the subject and have ascertained from him that it is not intended by the new arrangements to which you refer that the new Director shall be personally charged with architectural duties. I trust therefore that no change is intended to be made as to the duties which I have hitherto discharged as the architect employed on the building, responsible for all works of an architectural character carried on therein.

It was a bold stroke which struck home. Captain Galton, ambitious for office, had been brought in with the approval of Ayrton, but clearly knew nothing about architecture. Now Edward Barry had gone direct to the Chancellor of the Exchequer, who readily gave his reassurance to the architect without being fully aware of the office politics involved. Barry's letter went on to point out that the sudden removal from his post as the architect of the New Palace would be calculated to do him most serious professional injury, and in this he was undoubtedly right.

There are only two recognized reasons for immediate dismissal from any post in the public service. The first is for corruption, which means at lowest an official's fingers being caught in the till when a passing senior slams it shut, and at highest a more gentlemanly but fraudulent conversion of funds. The second reason is for flagrant immorality, such as an arrest for indecent behaviour in a public place. Inefficiency can never be a ground; there are rules entitling the offender to endless cautions before the stage of premature retirement is reached, and sometimes indeed it may lead to unexpected promotion, as with useless Ministers who find themselves kicked upstairs by the award of a barony.

Barry had not erred on any of these counts. Indeed he had proved himself far more expeditious than Sir Charles had been. He pointed out in his letter that even after completion of a major work, it is frequently necessary to retain a private architect on official attachment to prevent inexpert damage or disfigurement to the architecture. 'With my feelings respecting the New Palace of Westminster, as an artist, and as my father's son, I feel I should be wanting in my duty if I did not earnestly, though I trust respectfully, protest against any plan which may lead to the injury of a building which (whatever may be said against it) is at least one of the most remarkable architectural achievements of the nineteenth century.'

The peculiar circumstances surrounding the first letter from the Minister were unresolved by his brief reply to Edward Barry's pleading. Again, it consisted of two sentences, so abrupt as to compound the offensive quality of the first letter of dismissal. The second letter, dated 7 March, was as follows:

Sir,

Adverting to my letter to you of 22 January last, I am directed by the First Commissioner of Her Majesty's Works to remind you that no steps have yet been taken by you to place the plans and drawings of the Palace at Westminster in the office of the Clerk of Works.

The First Commissioner desires me to add that he has not thought it necessary to enter into any discussion of the topics raised in your letter of the 10th ultimo, based upon assumptions which he does not recognize, and he requests that you will be good enough to comply with the directions contained in my letter to you of 22 January last, above mentioned, before the close of the financial year, and that you will also be good enough to forward all the contracts or correspondence constituting them which at present remain unexecuted.

I am &c,

GEORGE RUSSELL
Secretary.

The additional request in this second letter relating to contracts served to demonstrate the uninformed hastiness with which the first letter had been sent from the Office of Works. If Captain Galton, the new Director of Works, was behind the affair, surely he should have known that an architect does his work with and through contractors and that they are answerable to him at all stages? Apparently this elementary fact was only now being appreciated. It enabled Barry to take a somewhat sharper line in the reply he sent a week later:

I have received your letter of the 7th instant. Considering that your letter of the 22nd January has been sent to me without a word of previous explanation, at a time when the First Commissioner is aware that several of the works officially entrusted to me are still unfinished, and considering the friendly relations with successive Ministers which it has been my privilege to enjoy during the long period in which I have acted as architect to the Houses of Parliament, I had expected that my letter of the

10th ultimo would, at least, have been considered by Mr Ayrton worthy of a reply, if not of his favourable consideration.

Barry went on to raise the question of uncompleted contracts. No architect who valued his reputation would leave work unfinished, once he had begun on it, and he was therefore 'compelled to ask for explanation on this point'. The other point related to the peremptory demand to hand over all drawings. These, he explained, were in two classes. In the first were those drawings which he had himself made during the past ten years. The second class contained the drawings and plans made during the lifetime of Sir Charles Barry. 'Many of these,' he wrote, 'are invaluable to me, being by his own hand, and they constituted his only bequest to me at his death; I therefore value them accordingly and regard them as a sacred deposit. I cannot believe that the First Commissioner will seek to deprive me of this much-prized inheritance.'

Three days later in the next reply from the Office of Works, there was a slight weakening of the earlier obdurate tone. The Minister would now allow Barry to exercise his own judgement in the first instance in assembling the plans, drawings and papers necessary to afford the Office of Works staff a complete knowledge of the Houses of Parliament. Meanwhile the papers of Sir Charles Barry could for the moment be retained in Edward's possession until the department had arranged an inspection of them and decided which he might be allowed to retain. The Office of Works admitted also that they had not kept copies of a number of contracts, of which they therefore wished to see the originals, and confessed that they did not know what contracts Edward Barry referred to, or when they had been forwarded to the Office. The question of Barry's further employment by the Office of Works would be held over until he had produced the plans as required, particularly the working plans and sections and specifications used in construction of the building and foundations, its embankments and sewers. The sewers again! These facts were vital for whoever succeeded the Barrys, for the intricacies of the past construction were producing strange effects within the building, and without the architect's plans and special knowledge it would be impossible to remedy them.

The secrets of the horse manure, for example, had only been

probed a couple of years before. For a long time the Commons had been puzzled by a curious ammoniac smell of horses' excrement which wafted through the debating chamber. That, of course, was no part of the architect's responsibility, but under the improved system of ventilation devised by Goldsworthy Gurney after the departure of Dr Reid, the air passed through gauze 'by which it was deprived of much mechanically suspended impurity', then over the warming apparatus known as 'Gurney's batteries' and finally into the House itself through its perforated floor. An expert had now traced 'the not very agreeable emanations from horse-dung'. The explanation was as simple as the remedy. Near the gauze-hung air inlet was the door to the Ladies' Gallery, and it was there that coaches waited sometimes for hours, in the course of which their horses might heed the call of nature. In the expert's official report the words are plainer: 'If horse-dung happens to fall near any of the inlets the air is contaminated. . . .' In future coaches were directed to wait in Speaker's Court and only to move forward to the door when called. Curiously, cars follow this strict routine to this day, although the Ladies' Gallery has gone and the horses themselves have long since galloped into history.

Edward Barry now pressed his advantage over the Office of Works. Why indeed should he return the plans to them? It was not, he argued, in line with previous Office of Works practice. He had submitted the case to the Royal Institute of British Architects and they had gone so far as to come to a resolution by the Council firmly asserting that all drawings and papers of an architect made for the purposes of erecting a building remained the sole property of the architect. The rules of the American Institute of Architects also declared that 'drawings, as instruments of service, are the property of the architect'. The co-executors of Sir Charles Barry's will had also entered the lists on Edward Barry's behalf. They had consulted Messrs Grueber and Cooper, solicitors for the will, of 5 Billiter Street in the City of London, who, speaking for the executors, declared that the highest authority had advised them that it was not possible for the documents to be surrendered.

Finally, Barry wrote that he had been informed by members of his own family that they would feel aggrieved 'if I surrender what they consider was left in my hands as a sacred trust, and the nature and tenor of all this, combined with my own feelings on the subject, place an insuperable barrier in the way of my handing over my inheritance to the First Commissioner of Her Majesty's Works'. He would, however, be ready to compromise so far as his own drawings were concerned, and allow the Director of Works to see them and to make tracings, at the expense of the Office of Works, of any they might need. This time the Minister's reply only took one day to prepare. It threatened to bring in the law: 'As you now, for the first time, repudiate the right of the Crown to ask for the plans and documents mentioned in my letter of 22nd January last, which have been prepared for the service of the Crown at the public charge, the First Commissioner has referred the correspondence to the solicitor for this department.'

Meanwhile, Barry's attention had been drawn to what seemed a piece of sharp practice by the new Director of Works, Captain Galton, which goes some way towards explaining the need for immediate access to the plans. In July 1869, some months before the present storm had broken, Edward Barry had prepared a plan for new refreshment rooms in the Commons and a new conference room for the Lords. It had taken him several years of study and negotiation, after which he had been called to give evidence before a House of Commons Committee on 2 and 4 August of that year. Now he found to his surprise that a new plan, copied in principle from his but without any mention of the fact, had been laid before a Committee by the Office of Works, and that his plan was stated to have been prepared by Captain Galton, but with some clumsy alterations to which Edward Barry was happy to draw attention. For example, the public entrance to the new conference or committee room was by an ascent of five steps succeeded immediately by a descent of five more; the proposed serving room was placed in one of the main corridors and was unprovided with any external light or air; the light of the ground-floor windows on the east side of the Peers' Inner Court was affected by columns placed in front of them to carry a projection above of eleven feet in width, and so on, mentioning several more gaffes. By this time the Office of Works had ceased any pretence of playing the game. The reply in this brief interlude of the bigger controversy was now reduced to a single sentence: 'I am directed to state,' wrote George Russell, 'that, without admitting the accuracy of your remarks, the First Commissioner declines to enter into any discussion with you respecting the proceedings of this office.'

It is difficult to explain the virulence with which Edward Barry was treated by the Minister in charge and the staff of the Office of Works. The occupational disease of politicians has been said by one of their number to be envy, and there was certainly plenty in Barry's recent work to excite that emotion.

Yet fear rather than envy might have provoked the hostility and the determination of the Office of Works to get rid of the last of the Barry connection. A staff that had not acted for more than seven years to check the deterioration of stone by the simple application of linseed oil, and which did not even show a full understanding of the role of contractors in architectural work, could not have borne the strain of a new major operation.

Disraeli's government in 1868 had not lasted twelve months, and the Office of Works might have feared that, in view of Gladstone's wild plans for reform, as many regarded them, the Conservatives might soon be back and the Barry mischief brought up again. The new Director of Works, utterly incompetent to regulate the contractors, could only see that the goings-on must be stopped by the removal of the progress chaser in Parliament, and the dust he and his father had been causing for generations might then be allowed to settle. The Minister, Ayrton, would have perhaps been influenced by similar anxieties, as parliamentary criticism would fall on him. There was, moreover, the open letter to Members of both Houses from Edward Pugin. It was written in 1867, and slow poison from that source must have begun to infiltrate the minds of some Ministers as well as back-bench Members.

Gladstone, as his later history vividly demonstrated, was an injustice collector in respect of public and private causes. He seethed over Macedonian massacres, and grieved over the morals of harlots on the newly built Victoria Embankment. He may have been sufficiently influenced by the knowledge of Pugin's wrongs to decide that if a member of his government thought that Barry should go, he would tacitly support the move, or at least do nothing to alter the harsh decision. In the meantime, relations between the architect and the Office of Works were moving to an open breach from which retreat was becoming impossible for either side. It was now to be a question of pitched battle ending in defeat for one side or the other.

Edward Barry was on stronger ground than his father had been in an earlier situation, since he could point to a building which now stood, larger than life, on the bank of the Thames opposite his own drawing office in Abingdon Street, created by a lifetime of work, alternating with every kind of frustration, by his father and himself. That he felt this bond keenly is apparent from every letter he wrote. At the same time, he was given stronger professional support than his father had ever received. Charles Barry had at one time been criticized for not maintaining the prestige of the profession in yielding too readily to the reduced fee imposed on him by the Office of Works, his main opponents in the early days being fellow architects. This time Edward Barry had gone at once to the Royal Institute and had been given their unqualified support in his struggle with the Office of Works.

The blow-for-blow character of the correspondence between Ayrton and the Office of Works on the one hand and Edward Barry on the other did not abate as the financial year approached its close on 31 March. This was the time by which the Minister hoped to see the last of the man whom he now regarded as thoroughly recalcitrant, and his impatience was demonstrated by italics. He demanded, in a letter of 23 March, that Barry should send urgently *not later than the 28th instant* certificates showing the amounts due to contractors for works under his direction at the Houses of Parliament, so that the contractors could all be paid off by the end of the month. Barry's reply was negative. He had already sent in all the certificates he intended to submit during the current financial year. Surely the Minister knew the principles of payment, he asked. The first was that certificates should not exceed the sums voted by Parliament for that year, and the second meant that 25 per cent of any payment to contractors was held over for three months as a safeguard against defects of workmanship. If the Minister wished him to issue further certificates without regard to these principles, he observed sarcastically, 'I shall be happy to receive his directions on the subject'.

Between March and May, half a dozen more letters flew to and fro between the adversaries. The Minister yielded ground on the issue of withholding 25 per cent, and consequently Barry carried on with the existing contracts. The royal staircase and the Queen's Robing Room were still unfinished, and Barry intended to finish them under the contracts already given out. By the end of May, the Office of Works was writing 'there has never been any question as to your duty to see the contracts duly completed, and to certify the balances payable under those contracts, and the First Commissioner therefore requests that you will be good enough to proceed with, inspect and certify the work in the usual manner.'

Edward Barry did not let matters rest quite as easily as that. He was determined to exact some sort of redress for the earlier discourtesies he had suffered. Accordingly he wrote back:

I am glad to find that, contrary to the conclusions drawn by myself and others from the previous correspondence, it is the wish of the First Commissioner of Her Majesty's Works that I should continue to superintend the completion of the unfinished works commenced by me. . . . With reference to your statement that there has never been any question as to my duty, I have to remark that no such question has been raised by me. If any doubts have arisen on the subject, they have been wholly caused by your letters to me. . . . The doubts would have been removed at once if the First Commissioner had then thought it right to reply to my questions respecting them.

In June hostilities were resumed. George Russell suspected that Barry was paying for staff as though all the arrangements were to continue as before. He therefore demanded an explanation of the circumstances under which a claim by a Mr Presland had been rendered for thirteen weeks' salary as the Clerk of the Works, and certified as correct by Edward Barry. The architect replied that Mr Presland's salary of three guineas a week was entirely correct, and he had certified the account as was customary. Back came a letter from the Office of Works asking how soon the services of the Clerk of the Works could be dispensed with, and when Barry expected to issue certificates for the completion of all works under his direction at the Houses of Parliament. There were further pinpricks. The

Serjeant at Arms of the Commons was evidently anxious to curry favour with the new powers at the Office of Works. Instead of going direct to the architect, he applied to the First Commissioner of Works for the heraldic lion and unicorn which had been removed some time ago from the back of his chair. It provided ammunition for another shot at Barry. 'These carvings being, as the First Commissioner understands, in your charge, he desires me to request that you will cause them to be delivered to Mr Fincham, the Board's Clerk of the Works at the Houses of Parliament.'

Edward Barry had had enough. On 9 August, the day after he received the complaint about the lion and unicorn, he wrote forwarding the final account and recommending payment of the balances due to the contractors, adding:

It is with no ordinary feelings that I find my present official connection with the Palace abruptly terminated, and the completion of my work entrusted to others. As architect to the building since my father's death in 1860, and accustomed from boyhood to give to it the foremost place in my thoughts, and to visit it almost daily, I cannot fail to retain a lively interest in all that relates to it. . . . I cannot notice without anxiety that important alterations and additions are about to be carried out from plans which, as it appears to me, have been taken from mine, but without, as I understand it, any further architectural advice. Under the circumstances, it may possibly be thought excusable if I note with satisfaction that, in the House of Commons, the Premier and the Chancellor of the Exchequer were pleased to refer to my past services in complimentary terms, and that all the ex-First Commissioners of Works under whom I have till now acted, have publicly testified that my duties at the Houses of Parliament have been discharged to their satisfaction, and in their opinion, not wholly without advantage to the public service.

He also regretted in this letter that certain artists had been approached to cope with his own unfinished designs for the Central Lobby without the chance being given him of taking any part in their deliberations. This was the only point on which the Minister deigned to authorize a reply. George Russell wrote:

With reference to that portion of your letter in which you comment on your not having been associated with the eminent artists who have been applied to by the First Commissioner respecting the works of decoration of the Houses of Parliament, I am to inform you that whilst, as already stated in my letter to you of the 29th June last, he declines to enter into any discussion with you respecting the proceedings of this office, he is of the opinion that no public advantage would result from associating you with the committee of artists who have been good enough to undertake inquiries with which, it appears to the First Commissioner, you have no concern.

It was hard for Edward Barry to be told these were matters with which he had no concern, and he protested at this curt dismissal:

I have been engaged in the public service during the whole of my professional life, and have endeavoured to complete my father's great work in a manner worthy of his reputation, and of the public. Considering the courteous allusions to myself used publicly by former First Commissioners, and by Mr Gladstone and the Chancellor of the Exchequer, I cannot but feel that I might have expected an answer somewhat different from that which I have received.

When it came to his dismissal, praise from the Prime Minister and Chancellor was tinged with somewhat odious hypocrisy. They appreciated his services to Parliament but were ready to allow his engagement to be prematurely ended, however unjustly, by a less senior Minister. The acrimony was diminished, but harassment still continued.

Barry's departure left unanswered the question of Sir Charles Barry's drawings. The Office of Works had now been advised by the Law Officers of the Crown (the Attorney General and Solicitor General) that all the papers, designs and documents necessary for affording a complete knowledge of the building were the property of the Crown, and should therefore be surrendered by Edward Barry. The architect might, however, be allowed to submit his father's drawings separately to ascertain whether copies of these might serve the purpose, instead of the originals. Barry's response to this new demand was to send the remainder of his own drawings to the Office of Works, to add to those of his plans already in the department's possession, and to propose that copies of his father's drawings, but not the originals, should be supplied. As he said, this seemed a reasonable solution to the question. While recognizing the high authority of the Law Officers on a point of law, he asked whether he could be given copies of the case submitted to them by the Office of Works and of their opinion on it. The reply was unexpectedly conciliatory. Although the Law Officers' opinion was confidential, the architect was told that he could submit a joint case for a new opinion by the Law Officers if he thought that all the facts had not been put forward by the Office of Works in their own submission. Edward Barry responded by saying that he would readily accept any fair proposal to decide the question. He pointed out, however, that the Law Officers had already expressed an opinion which was adverse to him; he suggested referring the question to some outside authority unconnected with the government, such as a retired judge. Once again the Office of Works were ready to meet his objection. Sir William Erle was a distinguished former judge, and when Barry put forward the name, there was no dissent. At that moment, however, an unexpected decision was reached by three judges in the Court of Exchequer on another case, in which it was ruled that an architect's drawings of a building belonged to the employer of the architect. Further resistance was useless in view of the High Court judgment, and Barry now indicated his willingness to surrender.

In his first courteous letter since the contest began, the First Commissioner 'learns with much satisfaction that you are prepared to deliver up to the Crown the documents mentioned in your letter', and promised that 'he will have a selection made of those which it may appear to him may be returned to you'. This sudden change to a tone of reason and courtesy probably resulted from the fact that the dismissal of Barry was being raised in the House of Commons, and an order made for the exchange of letters to be laid on the Table for the information of its Members.

Although the episode of Sir Charles Barry's plans seemed to be over, it was something which Edward Barry never forgot. He was only eighteen when he first entered Barry's office to assist his father. He could, like his father, have devoted his life to many other architectural projects. When in 1857 the Covent Garden Theatre had been destroyed by fire, he rebuilt the Opera House, as it stands today, in the short space of eight months. He was prolific in designing and building churches, hotels, country mansions, public libraries, schools and town halls throughout Britain. Charing Cross – the monument to Queen Eleanor and the hotel which stands behind – the Inner Temple buildings facing the Thames, and the Children's Hospital in Great Ormond Street illustrate the variety and success of his work.

The cavalier treatment he received through his dismissal and particularly through the government's demand for his legacy of drawings was deeply wounding. Writing of it later he said, 'it seems as if there was a dead set made against me, and I am tempted to quit a profession where such things are possible'.

In the end, the plans brought little benefit to the Office of Works. Whether they were mislaid, or whether the inexperienced Director failed to appreciate those which it was vital to preserve, remained a mystery for many years. Later architects employed by the Works Department found that there were no plans to help them in plumbing the depth between floors or within the great ventilating vaults left behind when the egregious Dr Reid made his exit. The unworthy rumour was put about that Sir Charles, indignant at being bilked of his fees, had destroyed the drawings before he died. It was not true. The upheavals of the Second World War led to the discovery in a house in Cheam, Surrey, of fifty-two drawings by Sir Charles Barry for building the Houses of Parliament. The householder, Mr Charles Marshall, generously offered them to the Ministry of Works, who found that some of the drawings were undoubtedly useful and retained them. The remainder were accepted by the Royal Institute of British Architects, marking a historical postscript to the proud day when in May 1850 the then President, Lord de Grey, presented Barry with the gold medal of the Institute, observing significantly, 'the means have been withheld, and difficulties have been unnecessarily created'.

CHAPTER NINE

DUST AND
DISORDER

1880

After the dismissal of Edward Barry, there were many years of comparative quiescence in the circles concerned with the parliamentary building. The Office of Works had no wish to become more closely involved than was necessary in any new schemes for the Palace of Westminster. The alternating governments of Liberal and Conservative seemed set in their courses and the political machine was turning over with well-oiled momentum. In 1868 Gladstone had displaced Disraeli as Prime Minister. In 1874 Disraeli had replaced Gladstone. Gladstone had come back as Prime Minister in 1880. Then in 1885, after Disraeli's death, the Marquess of Salisbury became Conservative Prime Minister. Gladstone returned to lead his third Liberal administration in 1886, and in the same year Salisbury took over again. Gladstone became Prime Minister for the fourth and last time in 1892.

There were problems enough in Parliament, culminating in the Irish Members' plot to wreck proceedings in the House, to override any building questions. In 1880 the Clerk of the House confessed in his private journal that the difficulties of parliamentary government were becoming more serious and his complaint that the Irish party in the Commons was 'disorderly and contumacious' was a mild understatement. It was not until 1894 that there was any serious move to look once more at the problem of accommodation and to consider enlarging the House. In that year, a Select Committee under

Herbert Gladstone reported that there was a marked difference of opinion on the subject, but by a narrow majority they turned down the idea of building a new debating chamber.

The revival of a demand for a larger House was explained by a Gladstonian reform bill of 1885 which by redistributing seats increased the number of Members from 632 to 670. The Committee did, however, extract three rooms from the Lords, with the courteous agreement of Lord Ancaster, the Lord Great Chamberlain. The generous allocation of rooms to various officials in the Commons also began to be reduced. The Speaker's train-bearer had four rooms for his own use. By comparison the space available for 'the gentlemen of the Press' and their large staff of messengers, who carried their reports to Fleet Street, altogether numbering 386, was quite inadequate. The Select Committee solved the problem without hesitation. The train-bearer, Mr French, could give up his rooms to the Chaplain and Ministers, and get an allowance in lieu. The Chaplain having been eased out of his room, *The Times* staff could move into it; the room previously occupied by *The Times* staff would then be converted into a lavatory.

All was plain sailing, but already two other innovations were made which, though minor in character, foreshadowed grave mistakes in planning. In the Commons Inner Court, one of the eleven courtyards in Barry's plan intended to give light and air, the width of open space was reduced in order to provide a servants' hall, a porters' room and a cigar room. Secondly, better accommodation was provided for sixteen maidservants, who occupied premises upstairs, by dividing one of their rooms and providing a bathroom. These two schemes, innocuous and even beneficial in themselves, set a precedent of incursion into the courtyards and splitting up of well-proportioned rooms which was later to be followed with ruinous effect on the design of the new Palace.

Following the death of the old Queen, Members' thoughts turned to their own condition once again. In 1902 Sir Archibald Milman died after only two years as Clerk of the House. A Member who had sat in five Parliaments had no difficulty in diagnosing the reason. Death, he claimed, was caused by the cellar-like damp and chilliness of the House at the beginning of every autumn and winter session. The building was disgracefully neglected during the long recesses. Dirt and dust accumulated in the draughty corridors, followed at last by a hasty clean-up before Parliament resumed. 'I suppose we shall have the usual sousing over of the tiles of the passages,' he grumbled, 'and meet the usual damp and steamy atmosphere which we as "human stoves" help to dry out at much risk to health. I have watched these proceedings for years,' he went on, 'the House and its committee rooms and passages are full of poisonous dust, probably charged with influenza germs.'

The departure of officials as well as of Members during the adjournments of the House was well recognized and indeed understandable. In the opening year of Edward VII's reign, there were still 3634 cases of typhoid fever and diphtheria, and 1356 cases of smallpox in London, and although there were several residences for officials within the Palace, it was good to get away. 'All these labours overtaxed my strength,' wrote a Clerk in Gladstone's day, 'and in the month of July I was fairly worn out. I was advised by Dr Herman Weber to try the Homburg waters and I was urged to start without delay. But this I could not do in the heat of the session without urgent necessity, so I waited until within a few days of the Prorogation, when I started for Homburg accompanied by my wife. Having spent the usual month at that gay watering place, water-drinking, promenading, dining and idling, we went to Switzerland and returned via Paris to England early in November, after an absence of nearly three months. My health was certainly improved, if not by the waters, by the rest and recreation I needed so greatly. Our autumn was spent partly in Town and partly in visits to Lord Eversley at Heckfield, Lord Egerton at Tatton, and other friends in the country.'

Away from Westminster the golden age may have been a reality. Neglect of Barry's Houses of Parliament and failure to institute a reasonable standard of service and of cleanliness now seemed to be a permanent part of its tradition, which would not be seriously challenged in the reigns of Edward VII, George V and Edward VIII. It was not until the reign of George VI that a new inspection was to take place, through the accident of war and its aftermath, and the burning, once again, of the House of Commons.

CHAPTER TEN

IN FLAMES AGAIN

1941

'Algie doesn't like bombs,' observed Mrs Speaker, explaining the preference of her husband, Captain Algernon FitzRoy, for getting away early from the House on the nights of the full moon. By one of those ironies in which fate is so prolific, Captain FitzRoy (his captaincy deriving from the Lifeguards) was in fact the only resident to die within the House of Commons throughout the whole war, not from enemy action, but from influenza in 1943. He was an austere but not unkindly man, only impatient if some ignorant clerk spelt his name with a small *r*. The surname FitzRoy implied a bar sinister of the highest lineage, and descent from a royal bastard was obviously a matter for greater pride than descent from a common one.

Throughout the last years of this Speaker's life, bombs rained down on and around the Palace of Westminster with remarkably little effect. On moonlit nights in particular, enemy bombers found no difficulty in tracing the line of the river Thames to London and releasing their loads on what seemed good targets, but barrage balloons on long steel hawsers discouraged low flying and made identification of individual buildings difficult. In September 1940 a high-explosive bomb, falling in Old Palace Yard, severely damaged the walls of the south and west front and Barry's great window at the south end of Westminster Hall, bending Richard Cœur de Lion's sword without unseating him from his enormous bronze steed.

The most serious damage to the Houses of Parliament was in the course of the biggest enemy raid on London on Saturday 10 May 1941, when the great building was struck a dozen times. The House of Commons Chamber was entirely destroyed by fire, and the famous roof of Westminster Hall was set alight. At one point Civil Defence had to make a dramatic choice of action.

'Let the pseudo-Gothic go. We must save the Hall,' cried Colonel Walter Elliot, an excitable and historically minded Member. Seizing a fireman's axe, he manfully struck at the great oak door to gain access. It was locked and time was lost because he failed to guide the firemen through the side door which was left permanently open for just such an emergency. The hammer-beam roof was saved, however, and in spite of current indignation over the barbarity of the onslaught on the very birthplace of parliamentary democracy, the records of the Luftwaffe show it was not a deliberate attack on the Houses of Parliament.

There is, moreover, a curious footnote to the history of the affair. Mr Kenneth Mackenzie, preparing a revised edition of his guide to the Houses of Parliament, found an architectural aside by a German author which referred in glowing terms to 'Barry's masterpiece, its thousand windows reflected in the waters of the river Thames'. He placed this as an apt quotation on the first page of the Official Guide to the Houses of Parliament, correctly attributing it to the author 'Adolf Hitler – *Mein Kampf*'.

Mr James Callaghan, who was then a newly elected Member of Parliament, was not amused and complained to the Speaker, who agreed that the quotation was inappropriate, and rather humourlessly instructed that a piece of paper should be stuck over the offending words. This was done, but the words still showed faintly through the paper, intriguing by their very obscurity. Finally it was decided to destroy all copies other than those already sold, which subsequently became treasured collectors' items.

The loss of the cramped debating chamber which Barry had so scorned was felt with nostalgic emotion by the older Members. There was much talk of Gladstone's fiery, if long drawn out, oratory when introducing a budget in a speech lasting over six hours, and of his great opponent's mellifluous wit, of which Barry himself was a butt when in 1850 Disraeli laughingly suggested to the House that they hang the architect:

No profession has ever yet succeeded in this country till it has furnished what is called 'an example'. For instance, you hanged Admiral Byng and the Navy increased in efficiency till we won Trafalgar. The disgrace of Whitelock was followed by the victory of Waterloo. We decapitated Archbishop Laud and thenceforward secured the responsibility of the bishops. The principle we have never yet applied to architects; and when a member of that profession is called on to execute a very simple task and has utterly failed, after a large expenditure of public money, it really becomes the Government to consider the case, and they may rest assured that if once they contemplated the possibility of hanging an architect they would put a stop to such blunders in future.

With the Commons debating chamber burnt out, Members were temporarily housed in Church House on the far side of the Abbey. It was here that Winston Churchill made some of his great wartime speeches, others being made in the House of Lords Chamber which was made over to the Commons for the remainder of the war. Churchill decided to press on with plans for rebuilding the parts of Parliament which had been destroyed, and in October 1943, when hostilities were reaching their climax, he demonstrated his versatility as wartime Prime Minister by making a finely prepared speech on the need to rebuild the Commons precisely as before.

For some time the British Broadcasting Corporation had been aware that these speeches from perhaps the greatest contemporary orator ought to be preserved. The text, of course, was printed in Hansard, but the technical service of the BBC was already capable of making perfect sound recordings. Mr Speaker Clifton Brown was approached for permission, and he in turn consulted representative opinion on both sides of the House. The response from Members was predictable: 'Whoever suggested when it comes to speeches that *he* was better than *me*?' The body of the protest from fellow Members was enough to alarm the new Speaker who obediently rejected the Corporation's request. The BBC returned to the charge. Could they make recordings of the speeches for the sake of history on the understanding that they would be left with the authorities of the House and never used in the lifetime of those concerned? The

Speaker replied that the matter had been decided and that there was no point in re-opening the discussion.

Churchill's speech about the rebuilding was memorable both for its delivery and because it reflected the sentiments of the overwhelming majority of the Commons at that time. They knew, as Churchill reminded them, that

if the House is big enough to contain all its Members, nine-tenths of the debates will be conducted in the depressing atmosphere of an almost empty or half-empty chamber. . . . We wish to see our Parliament as a strong, easy, flexible instrument of free debate. For this purpose a small chamber and a sense of intimacy are indispensable. . . . The conversational style requires a fairly small space, and there should be on great occasions a sense of crowd and urgency.

Next, he argued that there must be an oblong and not a semi-circular chamber, because the customary confrontation of parties facing each other was superior to any more logical system:

We shape our buildings and afterwards our buildings shape us. . . . The semi-circular assembly, which appeals to political theorists, enables every individual or every group to move round the centre, adopting various shades of pink according as the weather changes. . . . I have seen many earnest and ardent Parliaments destroyed by the group system.

Perhaps it was understandable when a humble but firmly non-conforming Member, Joe Tinker, vainly sought to interrupt the following stupendous flow of Churchillian rhetoric:

The vitality and the authority of the House of Commons and its hold upon an electorate, based upon universal suffrage, depends to no small extent upon its episodes and great moments, even upon its scenes and rows, which, as everyone will agree, are better conducted at close quarters. Destroy that hold which Parliament has upon the public mind and has preserved through all these changing, turbulent times and the living organism of the House of Commons will be greatly impaired. You may have a machine, but the House of Commons is much more than a machine; it has earned and captured and held through long generations the imagination and respect of the British nation. It is not free from short-comings; they mark all human institutions. Nevertheless, I submit to what is probably not an unfriendly audience on that subject that our

House has proved itself capable of adapting itself to every change which the swift pace of modern life has brought upon us. It has a collective personality which enjoys the regard of the public and which imposes itself upon the conduct not only of individual Members but of parties. It has a code of its own which everyone knows, and it has means of its own of enforcing those manners and habits which have grown up and have been found to be an essential part of our Parliamentary life.

The House of Commons has lifted our affairs above the mechanical sphere into the human sphere. It thrives on criticism, it is perfectly impervious to newspaper abuse or taunts from any quarter, and it is capable of digesting almost anything or almost any body of gentlemen, whatever be the views with which they arrive. There is no situation to which it cannot address itself with vigour and ingenuity. It is the citadel of British liberty; it is the foundation of our laws; its traditions and its privileges are as lively today as when it broke the arbitrary power of the Crown and substituted that Constitutional Monarchy under which we have enjoyed so many blessings. In this war the House of Commons has proved itself to be a rock upon which an Administration, without losing the confidence of the House, has been able to confront the most terrible emergencies. The House has shown itself able to face the possibility of national destruction with classical composure. It can change Governments, and has changed them by heat of passion. It can sustain Governments in long, adverse, disappointing struggles through many dark, grey months and even years until the sun comes out again. I do not know how else this country can be governed other than by the House of Commons playing its part in all its broad freedom in British public life. We have learned — with the so recently confirmed facts around us and before us — not to alter improvidently the physical structures which have enabled so remarkable an organism to carry on its work of banning dictatorships within this island and pursuing and beating into ruin all dictators who have molested us from outside.

At the end of it all, Churchill proposed that the House be rebuilt on its old foundations, using as far as possible its shattered walls. 'That,' he concluded, with shrewdly calculated bathos, 'is also the most cheap and expeditious method we could pursue to provide ourselves with a habitation.'

James Maxton, from Glasgow's slums, had a different and perhaps in retrospect a wider vision:

I should like to see premises built on a fine site, in good English parkland, as near London as that kind of land can be got; some twenty miles out, I should say, is not an impossible distance. There I would erect the finest building that British architecture can devise.

He proposed a special railway station in the grounds, with a fine car park, and even an aerodrome. Like most new ideas, however, it was airily dismissed by Captain Crookshank, who wound up the debate on Churchill's behalf:

I think it was one of the jests to which he [Maxton] sometimes treats the House. He outlined what seemed to be a glorified road-house some-where, a cross between the late Crystal Palace, a civil airport and Waterloo Station, situated in the surroundings of a Chatsworth.

After that rebuttal, Churchill's plan easily carried the day, by 127 votes to 3, with Maxton resignedly declaring that the Select Com-mittee might be composed of 'all the old deadheads of the House, if he so pleases'.

A Select Committee was then appointed to consider plans for rebuilding the House 'while preserving all its essential features.' It was not a remit which allowed much scope for experimentation. The Committee decided to rely on Sir Giles Gilbert Scott to design something appropriate. He was the grandson of the Gilbert Scott who in Barry's day had been woken by the 'thundering of Pugin's writings'. Unfortunately Sir Giles was a man of taste who eschewed the florid decorations of the original Chamber, and produced in-stead a muted reflection whose pastel colours tended to look washed out during the night sittings. New lighting was of a delicate daffodil shade, designed to give the impression of a morning in early spring, but Members' faces took on a ghastly yellow hue as though they were seated in a charnel-house. The galleries were enlarged to accommodate more visitors, but from most of the additional seats it was impossible to see much of the Chamber below. Acoustics were very poor but amplifiers were cunningly concealed in the carved Tudor roses which decorated the backs of the benches. As a result, listeners had to apply their ears to the back rail of each bench, giving a curiously contorted and soporific impression, rather remote from the Churchillian aim of 'a sense of crowd and urgency'.

Once again the defects were mainly the fault of his employers, for, like Barry, Scott had to meet their continuing call for Gothic. Fresh from designing the new sweeping Waterloo Bridge, he was required to provide plans in keeping with the Gothic style of the Palace. This dismal requirement was only tepidly endorsed by the Royal Fine Art Commission who approved Sir Giles's solution of the problem set him as dignified and satisfactory – 'working within the limits imposed'.

Lord Winterton, the chairman of the Rebuilding Committee, was an Irish earl, who for many years represented in the Commons a pleasant part of Sussex. He was tall and angular and would probably have agreed that his most outstanding quality, apart from physical courage, was irascibility. He did not suffer fools gladly and in a normal committee meeting he had been known to fly into a rage, demand that the room be cleared, turning out the witness and short-hand writer, to enable an angry challenge to be made against a supposed breach of order by some other member of the Committee.

During the Second World War, it was thought desirable to issue passes to Members, to guard against the unlikely but possible in-cursion of enemy aliens. The day chosen for the inspection of the new passes was, by chance, exceedingly wet, and the policeman on duty at the gates to New Palace Yard was soon in altercation with a furious gentleman who stubbornly resisted the man's gross imper-tinence in holding him up in the rain. Did he not know a Member of the House of Commons when he saw one? If he did not, what was he posted there for? Who gave him the authority to prevent a Member reaching the House? The reply that it was done on orders from the Lord Great Chamberlain did nothing to moderate the indignation of the protester, who was, of course, the Earl Winterton. The force with which he spoke ensured that never again during the remainder of the War was there any demand for Members' passes to be shown. It was, therefore, a surprise to him, as he confessed to the House, to find himself chosen as chairman of the Select Com-mittee on Rebuilding the House of Commons. He turned out to be an excellent one, presiding with skill and patience over long sittings, in the course of which thirty witnesses were heard in exhaustive detail.

A major disappointment, however, was the limitation put upon the Committee, first by the terms of reference drafted by the government, which required not some but all the features of the old House of Commons to be retained, and secondly by the Select Committee's own decision to adopt the strictest interpretation of their duty. They limited themselves to replacing the burnt-out Chamber, using additional space above and below it, and renewing any other accommodation that had been destroyed or damaged. These limits were made as much in the interests of traditional observance as they were for economy. At a time when war damage was widespread, a more generous scale of replacement could have been contemplated. As it was, the rebuilding cost about £2 million.

One of the Select Committee's main requirements was improvement of vision from all strangers' seats. This desire was duly carried out in the architect's plan, but as quickly nullified by the Committee's decision to enlarge both galleries and add a third row of seats to accommodate more strangers and pressmen. The result was to render a large section of the floor of the House frustratingly invisible to the unfortunate occupants of the additional seats. The seats in the Chamber itself were to be precisely the same as before, accommodating 346 Members out of a total of over 600, in order not to forfeit the quality of intimacy. The Committee were unanimous that the almost conversational style of debate could only be retained by a small debating chamber. 'The present intimate and traditional style of discussion is firmly established in the customs and affections of the nation.' The Lords Chamber was the same width as the Commons, but 12 feet 9 inches longer. The Committee were impressed by the noticeable diminution of the sense of intimacy produced by this slight difference in length. Some of the bolder spirits suggested an additional back row of seats, slightly widening the original Commons Chamber, but were outvoted by the more mature judgement of their colleagues.

On the vital question of ventilation, there was to be no return to the vertical draughts, upwards and downwards, of the old Chamber. The direction of the ventilation was to be lateral, by the alternation of gentle air currents; the plan was ahead of anything yet attempted. The Committee were not at first in favour of the permanently closed windows which the engineer, Dr Oscar Faber, had prescribed for the Chamber, and preferred to feel that these could be flung open to admit fresh air in fine weather. In the face of the explanation, however, that open windows are apt to short-circuit modern systems of air conditioning and to admit not fresh but dirty air, the Committee agreed that the high windows of the Chamber should be sealed. They were assured that the effect would be to reproduce in the Chamber 'all the atmospheric conditions of a warm spring day out of doors'.

There was a complete absence of the wrangling disputes between the Committee and the experts which had marred the history of the nineteenth-century building. Instead there were respectful exchanges of courtesies with those whom the Committee described as 'the best men available', and their report expressed confidence that when completed the building would be a House of Commons 'worthy of the Nation and the Empire'.

In the Commons debate that followed the presentation of the Rebuilding Committee's report, several Members were less certain about the wisdom of what was proposed. Churchill's arguments for return to the former shape of the House of Commons debating chamber were largely emotional. 'We have to look forward,' he said, 'to heavy party fighting when the House will be torn with fury and faction and full vent will be given to the greatest passions, when all the vocabularies may be used to the full.' He therefore declared it a matter of high public importance that they should sit as soon as possible in a House of Commons built on the old site. There were other Members whose outlook was more practical and whose desire for high passion and sparkling vocabularies was very much less than that of the Prime Minister. Doubts about the value of gladiatorial combat for the benefit of the public gallery were beginning to be entertained; the trouble was that the silent doubts were quite ineffectual when matched against convictions spoken in loud tones.

One of the essential features of the old Chamber was to be retained at the specific request of Churchill himself. 'I hope very much,' he said, 'that the archway into the Chamber from the Inner Lobby – where the bar used to be – which was smitten by the blast of the explosion, and has acquired an appearance of antiquity that might not have been achieved by the hand of time in centuries, will be preserved intact, as a monument to the ordeal which Westminster has passed through in the Great War, and as a reminder to those who will come centuries after us that they may look back from time to time upon their forbears who "kept the bridge in the brave days of old".'

Sir John Wardlaw-Milne, a vintage Tory of exceptional dignity, remained unimpressed. Two years earlier he had moved a vote of censure on Churchill's conduct of the war and suggested to an incredulous House that command of the forces be entrusted to HRH the Duke of Gloucester. Now he was critical of Churchill's emphasis on tradition and suggested instead that a new House of Lords could be built in the Victoria Tower Gardens. The whole Palace of Westminster would then become available for the Commons, enabling practically every Member to have his own room or to share one, as in the Parliament at Ottawa.

Although adhering to the old plan, Harold Nicolson proposed an advisory panel of Members to protect not only the responsible Minister but also the architects from what had happened to them in Barry's day. 'We do not want a repetition of those terrible interferences, interjections, interventions and bright ideas which brought Barry and Pugin to their graves. They were like the babes in the wood; they were buried and smothered under the falling leaves of bright ideas.'

Twenty years later, Nicolson's proposal was at last acted upon by the setting up of the House of Commons Services Committee. After thirty years the remedy proposed for the Commons of finding more room by moving the House of Lords has been tentatively put forward, but immediately rejected as unacceptably bold.

Major Peto, whose grandfather, Sir Morton Peto, had been the principal builder and contractor under Sir Charles Barry, had also an idea to voice which was then new, although reiterated in Parliament after Parliament in later years. Explaining that he was not making a plea for excessive comfort but for normal efficiency, he asked, 'Where can the ordinary common or garden Member of Parliament get his routine work done?' He felt a sense of shame at the impression which he and other Members created on visitors 'when they see the ludicrous position that exists; hon. Member after hon. Member huddled into some dark corner while he dictates to his secretary, who has two files and a notebook balanced on her knee'. Warming to his subject, he claimed that no board of directors, however small, would operate without an office, a typewriter, a telephone and some files yet 'we are the board of directors of the nation, conducting our business in a way which would be considered inefficient even for the organization of a troop of Boy Scouts, let alone the Mother of Parliaments'.

The constructive suggestion that he made, with all the force at his command, was at least for some sound-proof cubicles and a place to keep typewriters and files.

Clement Davies, later to become leader of the Liberal Party, and a thoughtful and devoted House of Commons man, made an even wider appeal. 'Are we really so limited in ideas that we have made no progress whatever since the old House was built?' he asked, recording once again the amount of work for constituents in writing and interviewing that has to be done outside the Chamber itself. Instead of a haphazard, slipshod scheme, which would be condemned by a later generation, there was a great opportunity to consider the whole question of the working needs of Members. It was pathetic, he argued, that 400 or more of those who did not live in London had to come up from their country constituencies to the House from Monday to Friday and search for such accommodation as they could find, often only a cheap bed-sitting room. All such matters, he pleaded, should now be considered by another more authoritative Committee, representing both Houses, and not limited to the narrow field of the present Rebuilding Committee. This brought Lord Winterton to his feet. In a moment he was horsed, spurred and away, asking the House in advance 'to accept his apology for having to put before it a somewhat intricate argument of a very delicate constitutional character'.

There were two men who purported to exercise authority over the Commons, neither of whom was subject to control by the House. The first, cast in the role of villain, was the Lord Great Chamberlain, the man on whose orders Winterton had once been stopped in the rain. The supporting player was the Serjeant at Arms. During the work of the Rebuilding Committee, one of its members desired to take some measurements in the Palace. It seemed a reasonable enterprise, and as a matter of courtesy the Clerk to the Committee, who himself ranked as an officer of the House of Commons, wrote to ask permission. He addressed his letter not directly to the Lord Great Chamberlain, since that personage was virtually unknown to those who worked in Parliament, and not even to the Secretary of the Lord Great Chamberlain, who was himself of fairly exalted lineage, but to Mr Meech, a less senior but more accessible official. 'Dear Sir,' replied Mr Meech, 'I am desired by the Secretary of the Lord Great Chamberlain to say he regrets that he cannot consent to the taking of measurements in the Palace of Westminster.'

Lord Winterton's anger was only partly moderated by the subsequent withdrawal of the prohibition. Nothing, he explained, should be taken as an attack on the distinguished persons who occupied these offices. It was purely a constitutional point, but the House ought to know where it stood. Was there not also that memorandum to the Committee by the Serjeant at Arms, who declared quite categorically that all the accommodation of the House of Commons was occupied and allocated by himself, as House-keeper, under an Act of the fifty-second year of George III's long reign? He had told the Committee quite bluntly, 'It is my statutory duty to allocate rooms, I could allocate the whole lot.' In the nicest possible way, Lord Winterton recalled another exercise of authority by the Serjeant at Arms which raised the whole question of accommodation for the Press. Members do not bear grudges but they have long memories. At one time, Winterton was editing a political and society newspaper, the *World*, and wished to have a Lobby and a Gallery representative. 'No,' said the Serjeant, and when asked if there was any appeal against his decision, he replied, 'None. The matter rests entirely with me.' These powers, concluded Winterton, ought really to be investigated. The remedy he and the Rebuilding Committee proposed was a small Select Committee, with perhaps Mr Speaker as Chairman, to look into the jurisdiction over the Commons exercised during their sittings by different authorities.

By this time, the debate on the Rebuilding Committee's report, the proposals for additional rooms for Members, the ideas for Clement Davies's large committee and Winterton's small one were all superseded by a new proposition. Arthur Duckworth, Conservative Member for Shrewsbury, felt it his duty to move an amendment denouncing the Gothic architectural design submitted by Sir Giles Gilbert Scott. He regarded the debate as one of supreme importance because the rebuilt Chamber, once constructed, might last for several centuries. With their responsibility towards posterity, it would be a very grave error to accept designs put forward by a single architect without giving younger men what might prove a supreme opportunity for new talents. The Chamber which was destroyed in 1941 had at least one very definite merit, continued Mr Duckworth: it was expressive and symbolical of the self-confident, opulent, tasteless years of the mid nineteenth century. The old Chamber was at least remarkable by its very robustness, its exuberance and its vulgarity. It probably had a most regrettable influence elsewhere; it was copied and exported to other parts of the world. This Chamber which the Rebuilding Committee offered 'will be third-hand Gothic in good taste. It will be a prim anaemic edition of the old Chamber. Will it have any influence anywhere else in the world? Will it ever be said by future generations that it was symbolic and expressive of our times?' The hon. Member went on to answer his own rhetorical questions: 'I say that to accept this design without any further consideration, without at least inviting other architects to submit their ideas, is to take the easy and defeatist course; it is to accept and admit that we are bankrupt of imagination, aesthetically dead, indifferent to the arts and indifferent to the claims of younger men.' A member of the Rebuilding Committee defended their work, observing that they had not been trying to build the Taj Mahal and quoting a Russian proverb, 'On taste and colour there is no comrade.'

At this point Lord Willoughby de Eresby, the Member for Rutland and Stamford, intervened with what has become a parliamentary by-word. Defending his father, the then Lord Great Chamberlain, who he admitted had very wide powers over the Palace, de Eresby said: 'It is almost a general rule of his office that any request is always refused the first time it is made. When it is made the second time, and is a reasonable request, it is always agreed to.'

Many more speeches expressed a general desire for additional rooms, and the Speaker, the occasionally testy Col. Clifton-Brown, impatient, ventured a couple of *obiter dicta* on his own account: 'It is impossible to imagine that over 600 rooms could be provided underneath the proposed Chamber,' he commented, and when a Member suggested building higher up, he added, 'That would probably mean a New York skyscraper, and I do not think it is worth the House's while to discuss that aspect.'

While most were for doing something, there were also powerful voices for doing nothing. Viscountess Astor, who represented heavily bombed Plymouth, was among them. 'Although we want to build a better and more beautiful House of Commons, there are things which are more urgent at this moment. I represent a much bombed place where there is a great shortage of houses. Let us not have a House which is built under the influence of a wartime consciousness, but let us look forward to a new generation with new ideas, a generation which will have more cooperation and less fighting. People on the front bench may like sitting on one another's laps,' she continued, 'and being jumped on, but it is terribly inconvenient for Members not to be able to get a seat and to have to crowd in and stand.'

Willie Gallacher, the Communist Member for West Fife, took the same view. The Commons were now temporarily installed in the House of Lords, where they were comfortable and working well. Indeed, he said, 'the significance of red benches seems to have an effect on people, even shell-backed Tories'. Surely nobody could claim that there was any need for priority for the new building compared with the importance of providing houses so that people could do their jobs, and, in his opinion, every bit of material and labour should be devoted to that purpose.

None of the various alternatives put forward in January 1945 were sufficiently supported to carry the day against the recommendations of Lord Winterton's Committee. The Minister of Works (Mr Duncan Sandys) dismissed the 'rooms for all' demand by pointing out that the Committee's plan already provided the maximum accommodation which could be managed without disturbing the skyline, and that to provide 615 small rooms would necessitate the building of another eight floors above the level of the roof of the Palace. 'And that,' interposed Mr Kirkwood, 'would be a real Tower of Babel.'

At the end of the long day's debate, winter darkness had fallen, and the war against Germany and Japan was still a grave distraction. The flying bombs of the previous autumn had damaged slightly or seriously one million out of a total of 2½ million houses in London. The battle of the Ardennes had temporarily shaken the allied front in Europe, resulting in 46000 American dead. There were still 2000 German tanks in the West, operating outside their own frontiers, and the Russian offensive in the East had not yet begun. Hitler's euphoria at military conferences towards the end of that month was noted by a despairing Albert Speer. Churchill and the dying Roosevelt were to confer on 4 February at Yalta with the jubilant Stalin and concede him Poland and the other eastern territories under promise of free elections everywhere.

It was not surprising that the decision of the House was to proceed without further investigation with the plan before them, rather than delve into other solutions at that stage. Curiously, the proposal which included rooms for interviewing constituents and other strangers on the lowest floor below the new Chamber was the only one which passed without comment. It was not until 1975 that the House of Commons Services Committee pointed to a danger which since the Gunpowder Plot of 1605 should have been in every Member's mind.

CHAPTER ELEVEN

A MEDIEVAL
HINDRANCE

1944

While the future reconstruction of the Commons was being canvassed, the builders' cranes were already swaying unsteadily around the House of Lords. The exterior stonework of the Victoria Tower was in a poor state of repair, and scaffolding erected in 1936 was tactfully left up during the war years to guard against a collapse of the Tower during air raids. It was not an unlikely chance. In one of the earliest raids, the church in Smith Square, a couple of hundred yards away, had received a direct hit, and great chunks of eighteenth-century stonework were thrown down on to the streets and pavements of the neighbourhood. On the top of the Tower was an observation post, useful for signalling a 'purple warning' or 'danger imminent', during daylight alarms, of which the legislators in the debating chambers below took less and less notice, since they had no air raid shelters to go down to, except for lower ground floor offices protected by sandbags.

The scaffolding did, however, fulfil a useful function on one particular night when fire bombs were falling in clusters during an enemy raid. One of the fire bombs lodged between the steep roof and outer parapet at the top of the Tower; as it burnt fiercely it threatened not only to start a big fire within the Tower, but also to act as a beacon for incoming bombers. Unfortunately, the Air Raid Precautions officer was off-duty, and the key to the Tower giving access to its iron spiral staircase was not immediately available. Sergeant Forbes, a Metropolitan police officer attached to the Palace, saw a way round that difficulty. Seizing a sandbag, he climbed over 300 feet up the scaffolding on the outside of the Tower and finally reached and put out the fire bomb. It was a great feat which was recorded with diagrams of the astonishing climb in the press. Many regretted, however, that in the stress of war the act was not officially recognized, and the gallant police officer never received so much as a letter of thanks from those in theoretical charge of the Palace at that time.

When a Labour spokesman asked at a Blackpool Party Conference for 'this medieval hindrance to progress to be taken off the backs of the people', he was perhaps unfair to the leaders of the Lords, since they were normally experienced former Members of the House of Commons, who were able, without having any longer to act as unofficial welfare officers to 50000 constituents, to devote more time and thought to the major affairs of the nation.

Now that the war was drawing to its close, a Joint Committee composed of Members of both Houses tried in October 1944 to look more broadly into questions of accommodation, in addition to the more limited problem of the bombed Commons. Their inquiries soon became channelled into an examination not so much of the whole building as of the individual houses and residential family flats which had been set up within it.

Viscount Simon, the Lord Chancellor, was examined about his problems of living in the Palace. His replies may be taken as typical of residents' reactions if asked to give up some of their homes within the building. 'I wish to express to the Committee my very strong view that it is in the public interest that the Lord Chancellor should have a residence in the Palace of Westminster,' he began in uncompromising tones. He then made a sortie against another resident, implying in him both limpet-like qualities and cowardice in the face of the enemy. It was all done in the smoothest manner of the great advocate which Lord Simon was. 'I had the good fortune for about two and a half years, I think it was,' he said, referring to the most desperate years of the bombing of London, 'to live in the flat which I have now returned at his request to Lord Esmé

Gordon-Lennox. I am raising no complaint about that at all, because before I came on the scene he had, as I understand, been allotted those premises, and I can quite appreciate that the Secretary to the Lord Great Chamberlain ought to live on the premises so that at any rate I am making no point about that whatever.' Describing the vital importance of his work as a member of the Cabinet who might be summoned at any minute to advise the Prime Minister at No. 10 Downing Street, or to sign documents such as the immediate need for the Great Seal to be put on some appointment, he continued his protest against the rival resident. 'The real position is that the authorities, whoever they were, finding the flat was not being used by successive Lord Chancellors, offered it to and made it the official residence of Lord Esmé, and that was the situation I found. The only reason I ever got in there myself was because he and his wife did not want to live there under war conditions, and my own arrangement with him was that he would let me use it on the understanding that I respected his superior right. This is quite right and I do not mind at all.' Underlining once more Lord Esmé's absence from duty when the war was hot, he added, 'As I have said, I have not the smallest complaint that I should be giving it up now, because that was my bargain with Lord Esmé. He did not wish to occupy it when the war was rather intense in London, and he has asked me to treat it now on the basis that the war for practical purposes is over; well, at any rate the bombing is over, and I do not raise any question at all. I am quite content and very grateful to him for having let me for the time being occupy the blitzed premises. But I am speaking of the future and I am quite certain that you ought not to omit the need of keeping the Lord Chancellor on the spot. That is all I wish to say.'

Within a few minutes the Committee were hearing a rather different story from Brigadier-General the Lord Esmé Gordon-Lennox KCVO, CMG, DSO, himself.

'May I tell the Committee to start with,' he began, 'that really all the rooms in this building are held by the occupier under a warrant signed by the Lord Great Chamberlain.' Before the war, Lord Chancellors did not live in the building, so Simon was something of a cuckoo in the nest. The warrant included the Houses of

Commons with the debating chamber and all other rooms because all were within the Palace of Westminster, which is lent by the Sovereign. 'The only room we do not touch is Mr Speaker's,' he added. As for Westminster Hall, that had always been rather a bone of contention between the Lord Great Chamberlain and the Office of Works. The Lord Great Chamberlain maintained he had charge of it, while the Minister of Works asserted his right to the authority formerly exercised by the Keeper of the Great Hall of Westminster.

'Who in fact controls it?' asked a Commons Member.

'We have in fact sort of smoothed it over,' replied Lord Esmé.

It would need an Act of Parliament to decide the issue.

The main dispute was then brought up.

'Would you say the Lord Chancellor had any historical right to the flat here?' asked Mr Geoffrey Mander, a famous Commons interrogator once denounced by Neville Chamberlain for 'his restless, mischievous curiosity'.

'None at all,' retorted Lord Esmé. 'The flat the Lord Chancellor is using now was servants' quarters when the Clerk of the Parliaments lived in the house, and above that again there were other rooms. Some of them are very fine rooms indeed, right up above, but they are frightfully dark, and there is no heating in them. I have never occupied the rooms at all; they are too many.'

It was, however, essential for himself to live on the premises. He did not see how he could do the work without being here. Some pertinent questions by the Committee then showed up the extent of his knowledge.

'How many people have you got under you, Lord Esmé?' inquired Viscount Mersey.

'I have got all the police, and all the custodians come under me, and the messengers and in some cases people in the Ministry of Works,' came the airy reply.

'A total of how many – fifty?' asked the noble Lord.

'More than that. I have got forty custodians alone; I should think forty or fifty police and the rest I could not tell you offhand, without going into it.'

Lord Southwood came to his rescue. 'It would be about a hundred all told?'

'Yes, very nearly a hundred,' agreed Lord Esmé.

There were many fascinating sidelights on the use of the building. The Clerk of the Parliaments at the turn of the century had a large and spacious house resembling that of the Speaker. There he lived and entertained, occupying the whole house from basement to roof, accurately described by Lord Simon as 'an appalling white elephant'. There were twelve main bedrooms alone. It was from the vast rooms of this house that a six-room flat for the Lord Chancellor was now being carved out of servants' quarters, at the end of which was 'a large sort of glass-house, a drawing room with an enormous expanse of glass' which Viscount Simon and his wife never used.

Apart from the original occupants, there were now all sorts of 'other little people, like the housekeeper, the senior engineer and so on', whose presence at night had for one reason or another been found essential. A Commons Member then gave evidence. He was, in fact, a hostile witness, Sir Herbert Williams, who had long advocated the end of what seemed to him an absurd system. 'This is a Royal Palace,' he explained, 'the Lord Great Chamberlain looks after it on behalf of His Majesty, but then a whole lot of other people come in. The Lord Chancellor has certain jurisdiction. Then under him is I think the Yeoman Usher of the Black Rod, who seems to act for the Lord Great Chamberlain. Then there is Mr Speaker who has jurisdiction if the House of Commons is sitting. If the House is not sitting the Lord Great Chamberlain's jurisdiction prevails. Then there is the Serjeant at Arms who looks after the washerwomen, the policemen and the custodians; and the Office of Works controls the man who works the lift, does the repairs, and sees to the taps, the lamps and the blinds. When we step from the Palace into Westminster Hall, the Lord Great Chamberlain's writ ceases to run, and the Minister of Works has jurisdiction there. They are physically one building, but in fact they are two buildings. I regard the thing as a great big joke, and how it has gone on all this time I cannot understand.'

He had seen eight rooms on each of eight floors in the Victoria Tower – sixty-four rooms in all.

'They are full of dust and documents. There are masses of Acts of Parliament, all beautifully written out by hand, and parchments covered in dust. I do not think anybody has touched any of them for years. Every one that I have seen is kept in the most disgusting condition and should bring discredit on somebody.'

This was not the way to speak to a Joint Select Committee of both Houses. Lord Esmé's evidence was more to their taste. The Chairman Earl Stanhope, asked him to reassure them, 'You do not think anything can be done to the Victoria Tower, do you?'

'Nothing at all,' said Esmé.

'Sir Herbert Williams is always talking about it as a waste of space?'

The reply was even blunter. 'I do not think so – he had better go and live there!'

Lord Southwood: 'It is an impossible place.'

That verdict ended the hope of any immediate changes in the Tower. The Committee were told that it would practically require gutting to make it habitable. Most of the windows had been blown out; there was no heating, no lift and no proper lighting, and it was almost inaccessible from any other part of the building.

On the more general question of spare rooms, Earl Stanhope observed that 'the allocation of accommodation seems to work very well on the whole', to which Sir Herbert Williams replied, 'It seems to me to work deplorably, because we have not got the accommodation, although I know there is a great deal of idle accommodation in this building.'

CHAPTER TWELVE

REBUILT IN THE
OLD FORM

1950

When the Chamber was destroyed on 11 May 1941 it could not have been foreseen that Sir Giles Gilbert Scott would have completed its replacement in time for the Commons to return on 26 October 1950.

There was not much decency in the manner in which the Victorians took up their residence in Barry's Chamber. Bernal Osborne, a well-known Member at that time, suggested that the House should be taken down and re-erected in Hyde Park as a better home for the Great Exhibition than the Crystal Palace. Another Member thought the House was well suited to be an aviary and all it required were a few canaries to twitter in the roof. There was cheap laughter at Barry's expense.

In 1950 the Members' attitudes were different and almost deferential. When the time came for the Commons to return from their temporary debating Chamber in the Lords, and their earlier and even more temporary one in Church House beyond the Abbey, the architect of the rebuilt Chamber was mentioned by name by the Prime Minister, Clement Attlee, and a number of workmen sat in the gallery, in company with twenty-eight overseas Speakers, the Lord Mayor of London, the Headmaster of Westminster School and Neville Chamberlain's widow. The celebrations did not end in the Commons Chamber. Because the King, George VI, could not enter the House due to constitutional objections raised when his ancestor, Charles I, was rash enough to do so, the Commons adjourned to Westminster Hall to present an address of thanks to him for the new Chamber. At a time when the margarine ration was still restricted to four ounces a week, the ceremony was one which brought a welcome return of splendour to the one-time banqueting hall, as a feast for the eyes if nothing more.

At the North Door an awning, furnished with a crimson pelmet and trimmed with gold braid, was erected, and the floor of the Hall was covered with felt. A pair of royal blue velvet curtains trimmed with gold were hung in Barry's great arch. On the upper dais, below the south window, two gilt chairs in the style of Louis XVI, upholstered in crimson damask, were set up for the King and Queen. Two heraldic beasts in gold and silver held escutcheons of the royal armorial bearings, trumpeters of the Royal Horse Guards paraded in gold embroidered tunics and blue velvet peaked caps, and the Commonwealth Speakers, in assorted robes and full-bottomed periwigs, added further shades to the scene.

The Commons Speaker tendered 'our most grateful thanks to your Majesty for having caused the rebuilding, on the same site, of that Chamber in your Palace of Westminster which was allocated for the use of the Commons by your royal predecessor Queen Victoria nearly a hundred years ago, and which was destroyed by the malice of your enemies in 1941'.

In his answer, the King said, 'The new Chamber has been built as far as possible in the form of the old. There is a traditional intimacy about our legislative Chambers which is very characteristic of Parliamentary life in our land. It suggests a close and almost homely place of discussion and taking counsel, as if it derived some of its virtue from the family circle. I am glad to know that this feature has been preserved in the new building. I congratulate the architect who designed the Chamber and all the men and women who have taken part in its building and furnishing. Its decorations and fittings are outstanding examples of our skill and craftmanship in wood and metal and stone.'

As he drove back to Buckingham Palace under a pale autumn sun the King was obviously happy in the knowledge of work well done, but it was not the beginning of contentment within the Palace of Westminster.

It was in 1953 that the Members of the House of Commons began to lose patience. Their votes provided the finance for all the buildings and all the services under the flag as big as a tennis court which fluttered from the pole seventy feet above the Victoria Tower. In spite of the researches of the Joint Committee at the end of the war, the impression lingered that among the 1100 rooms, it must be possible for a Member to find more than a single locker for his papers in one of the corridors.

A great conflict with the dictators of Europe had ended after six years with their unconditional surrender. It was surely not beyond the ability of the new and brighter intake of Members, many of whom were more versed in matters of war and peace than any of their predecessors, to succeed where Sir Herbert Williams had failed, and transfer to their own needs some of the premises occupied by those whom they generically described as 'the other users of the Palace'. It was a bold beginning that was needed, with a man in the chair of the Committee who would stand no nonsense. This was to be Mr Richard Stokes, a go-ahead business man from Ipswich, whose firm Ransome & Rapier was famed wherever farmers gathered to buy agricultural machinery. He was confident that it was an easy furrow he had been given from which to hoe a few weeds, and was only slightly dismayed when, telephoning at 11 a.m. to speak to the Committee Clerk, he was informed of his temporary absence after slipping on a cake of soap in the bath.

In the opening session of their inquiry, the Stokes Committee decided first to look into the question of accommodation and then to consider the appointment of officials who were taking up so much of it. In their first fifteen meetings the Committee examined a heavy phalanx of staff. In addition to one of the great officers of state, the Marquess of Cholmondeley GCVO, the Lord Great Chamberlain, they heard evidence from the Rt Hon. William Morrison MC, QC, Speaker of the House, Sir Frederic Metcalfe KCB, Clerk of the House, Brigadier Sir Charles Howard KCVO, DSO, the Serjeant at Arms, Major General Ivor Hughes CB, CBE, DSO, MC, Deputy Serjeant at Arms, Lieutenant-Colonel Sir Ralph Verney Bt CB, CIE, CVO, Mr Speaker's Secretary, the Hon. Sir Albert Napier KCB, QC, Clerk of the Crown in Chancery and Permanent Secretary to the Lord Chancellor, and others hardly less eminent, ending up with quite junior, but no less esteemed staff such as Miss Doris Date, Welfare Representative of the House of Commons Refreshment Department.

The result of their inquiry was to impress the Committee with 'the seemingly disproportionate amount of space at the disposal of the other users of the Palace'. To take one example from their report, they recommended that 'the bathroom on the third floor of the new building could be put to other use with advantage'. The plans had brought to light the existence of a Clerks' bathroom.

'Why,' asked the chairman, 'do the Clerks want a bathroom on the third floor of the House?'

'I have not the slightest idea,' replied Sir Frederic Metcalfe, who was momentarily taken aback, 'I cannot imagine how that slipped into the plan. The plans were considerably changed, you know, by negotiations with Sir Giles Gilbert Scott.'

'This is part of the new House, is it?' inquired the Chairman.

'Yes,' said Sir Frederic, 'that is the one. The bathroom, I have learned today, does exist. I have never been into it. I have not seen it myself, but it does exist near the lift. There are two little pantries. I think one has a gas ring in it, and I think the other only has a place for brooms and brushes.' Sir Frederic was anxious to prove he normally had an eye for detail.

'Is there a bath in it?' asked the Chairman.

'In the bathroom I am told there is a bath.'

'Does anybody bath there?' said Mr Stokes, not satisfied and continuing to press the witness.

'I am sorry, Sir, I do not know. People sometimes sleep up there on chairs or office furniture.'

'So,' exclaimed Mr Stokes, 'it is not really an important acquisition to your department?'

'I cannot help thinking,' said Sir Frederic, 'that it is largely a wasted bathroom.'

Viscountess Davidson intervened: 'Who are the other people up there? I expect they do use it when they change or anything.'

'No,' replied Mr Stokes, 'I have been through all that. I just wanted to know whether there was an active interest in it.'

There is no doubt that in a parliamentary democracy, moves are cautious rather than swift. All those concerned in the exchanges over the bathroom are no longer in the Commons. Only the bathroom remains as a mute witness to what might have been.

The Committee turned next to the functionaries in the House of Lords. By one of those ancient quirks of the constitution, the Speaker of the Lords is also Lord Chancellor, who as President of the Supreme Court of Justice has many aides who are not engaged in parliamentary duties, but who form a miniature government department inside Parliament. Why then should these people be taking up rooms which might otherwise be available to Members of Parliament?

'Would it really be administratively impossible for him to have a ministerial office outside this building?' inquired Sir Herbert Williams, who as a Member of the Stokes Committee had now returned to the charge.

'It would be entirely impossible,' responded Sir Albert Napier, the Clerk of the Crown in Chancery and Permanent Secretary to the Lord Chancellor. 'He has a great many staff outside but he must have a nucleus inside. The Lord Chancellor,' he explained, 'has to be near the Woolsack and the nucleus of his staff for all his administrative purpose has to be near him.'

The argument did not quite convince Members of the Committee. They could not believe it was absolutely necessary for thirty-five or more rooms in the House of Lords to be taken up by public servants who might do the work equally well outside in some office building. The Secretary of State for Scotland, for example, had a concentration of his departments in Edinburgh and a nucleus of a staff in London, but nobody had ever suggested that as a Minister and Member of Parliament he should have staff inside the Palace of Westminster.

'Are you putting to us,' asked Mr Charles Pannell, 'that it is almost administratively impossible for the Lord Chancellor to sustain his office without this; is it really so that there has to be personal consultation with the Lord Chancellor on all these points?'

'Yes,' replied the witness, 'a tremendous proportion of the Lord Chancellor's duties is choosing people for judicial jobs, nearly all the judicial jobs in the country, and that is very much a personal job. It would be a great mistake if you had a Department away from him who were in effect doing the choosing for him.'

The Committee were as pertinacious as they had been earlier over the Clerks' bathroom. How many appointments a year of judges, magistrates and so on did the Lord Chancellor make personally? It was soon apparent that the names of 1200 magistrates came up to him as recommended by city or county advisory committees, and the personal appointments were less than three or four a day.

'Take a normal day,' Mr Daines, another Commons Member sought enlightenment from Sir Albert Napier. 'I take it that most of the outside duties of the Lord Chancellor, his main duties apart from the Chamber, are carried out before the Chamber starts to sit. Would that be so?'

'Oh, no,' Sir Albert expostulated, 'We often have to talk to him on the Woolsack.'

'On the Woolsack?' Mr Daines was puzzled.

'Yes, he comes off the Woolsack,' explained Sir Albert.

Mr Daines still did not understand.

'You snatch a few minutes with him on the Woolsack for a major decision?'

'Yes,' was the reply, 'if anything is urgent and he often comes off for urgent meetings.'

'You seriously tell us,' persisted Mr Daines, 'that while he is actually sitting, presiding over their Lordships' House, he makes an important decision in conversation? You tell us that?'

'Well,' conceded Sir Albert, 'he comes out into the Prince's Chamber. . . . It is very often urgent.'

'It is incredible to me,' concluded Mr Daines.

At this point, Mr Richard Stokes intervened to give his own impression: 'I find it awfully difficult to accept that it is absolutely necessary that the Lord Chancellor's Department must have thirty-six rooms. I find it awfully difficult to accept it. Of course I do not question that that is a view which you sincerely hold, but some of the Committee – I am not speaking for the whole Committee but for myself particularly – might find it awfully difficult really to accept that the Lord Chancellor must have a staff which occupies thirty-six rooms in the Palace of Westminster when the place is simply chock-a-block and there is not enough room for Members of Parliament. Please do not misunderstand me,' he went on, 'I am not questioning for one moment the size of your staff. I am only questioning the essentiality of having them in the Palace of Westminster. That is what I find difficult to understand.'

'I am sorry you take that view,' Sir Albert replied firmly. 'In my opinion it is essential. Of course I have had to prove my case to the responsible authorities. I have had to prove what staff I needed and I have had to prove what accommodation I wanted and got. I think, if I may say so, the successive Ministers of Works and the Lord Great Chamberlain have been helpful and skilful in giving us accommodation which enables us to do our functions in adequate accommodation, which infringes as little as possible on what would be of real use to Members of Parliament.'

In their Report, the Committee made no recommendation to move the lawyers out of the building unless it could be claimed that they were included in the general dissatisfaction contained in the phrase: 'the existing situation calls for early improvement'.

Many years later, Mr Richard Crossman, who had been a Leader of the House of Commons in the 1960s, declared after he left office that the best solution for the accommodation problems of the Commons was to get the Lord Chancellor's large legal staff to move over to the other side of Parliament Square. They have not done so, and Sir Albert Napier's view of their essentiality has been accepted by successive Lord Chancellors. The Committee tried once more, in their examination of Sir Robert Overbury, the Clerk of the Parliaments, to investigate the use of rooms in the Lords. His department, he told the Committee, numbered fifty-one persons with forty-three rooms allocated to them. The Committee failed to shake him. Surely he did not need all that number of rooms?

'I would say it is adequate, but not too liberal.'

Again he pointed out that the Lord Great Chamberlain was responsible for the allocation of accommodation.

It was, therefore, with intense interest that the Committee waited to see the man who appeared to be the real power behind the scenes, and to whom every witness had referred them, the Lord Great

Chamberlain himself. When the Marquess of Cholmondeley appeared to give evidence in person, the Committee had expected at least some asperity and clash of wills. In the event, he quite disarmed them when he began his evidence.

'To be perfectly frank I have only been here for a year and a half,' he told them. By some accident of inheritance, absolutely clear to the College of Heralds but obscure to the general public, the hereditary office of Lord Great Chamberlain rotated among three noble families. It was no good blaming the Marquess of Cholmondeley for any bad decision taken by his predecessor, the Earl of Ancaster; and who could blame Ancaster, when it was probably in Lewisham's time that the original misjudgement was made? The Viscount Lewisham, in any case, would have had to have the royal agreement, and that would have been not in Queen Elizabeth's but in Queen Victoria's time. As for the Clerks, King Edward III had given privileges to the first of them in the Commons in 1363, but of course the Chancery Clerks in the Lords were well established long before that time, and even the Serjeant at Arms could claim rights of appointment dating from Richard II, whose Clerk of the Works was Geoffrey Chaucer, when the new roof was being built on Westminster Hall.

Lord Cholmondeley was soon leading the Committee into an examination of his own difficulties rather than into those of Members. He knew that regulations made in his name were always being quoted to inhibit Members' activities, and he knew that this caused irritation. Members taking parties of visitors round were constantly being stopped and told they could not go in a certain direction, by orders of the Lord Great Chamberlain. There was, said Lord Cholmondeley, no need for misunderstanding. The regulations for visitors were all in printed form. It was one of his unpleasant duties to see that the regulations were carried out. 'For example, last Saturday in our Lobby suddenly I saw a crowd of people, thirty or so of them, coming alone. I did not know they were with a Member. A Police Inspector was there and I said to him, 'Is not this wrong?' He said, 'Of course it is wrong. They are going against the grain.' If several Members are taking round parties against the grain, you get a funny situation. . . . I do not know how many thousands there were in the Prince's Chamber last Saturday who went against the grain.'

The Committee accepted the force of his argument and let him complete his evidence without any criticism. They were beginning to learn that in a true parliamentary democracy such as that at Westminster, there was no official with absolute authority, nobody wholly in charge and nothing to single out for condemnation except perhaps the inability of Members themselves to achieve what they wanted simply by acting collectively. They were not required themselves to do the work. All that was needed from them was an authorization of perhaps four lines on a piece of paper to be tabled and voted on. It was something which, year after year, remained beyond the capacity of Members of all parties.

The Stokes Committee were not making the strides they had anticipated when their inquiry began. They were in deeper waters than they had reckoned on, amateur investigators beginning to lose their footing in a swirling sea of titles and functions. How easy it was to confuse the Serjeant at Arms with an entirely different character, the hyphenated Serjeant-at-Arms in the Lords. Apart from attending upon the Lord Chancellor with the Mace, the latter's duty was minimal. So minimal was it that a quarrel resulted from the Gentleman Usher of the Black Rod's attempt to do it himself instead of leaving it to the Serjeant-at-Arms. This duty was to arrest delinquents upon an order by the House of Lords, a very rare function unknown in modern times. The unfortunate dispute between the two distinguished officers came to a head when the Lords had to step in as a body and resolve, on 9 July 1660, that on such an occasion they 'do reserve the power to themselves, to employ what persons they shall think fit'. The old enmity was not happily resolved until New Year's Day in 1971 when the office of Serjeant-at-Arms was taken over by Black Rod, so that one man alone embraces the disputed function.

The Stokes Committee began to see that it was futile to pin blame on the door of the Lord Great Chamberlain's often empty office, when in fact he was only marginally responsible for what went on in the Commons. It was equally difficult to find fault with the Serjeant at Arms, who under statute of 1812 was the Commons'

Housekeeper and responsible for its cleaning, except when a ladder involved the Works Department staff; they were answerable to a Minister of the Crown for the fabric of the building and for heights above the reach of a cleaner's hand. Like the Gentleman Usher of the Black Rod in the Lords, the Serjeant at Arms in the Commons holds a royal appointment, one of the few remaining in the personal gift of the Sovereign, although the House may remove him for misconduct. Every day when the House is sitting, the Serjeant is required to wear black silk stockings, silver-buckled shoes, a cutaway but collarless tail coat, a stiff but tie-less starched collar and a splendid rapier in a white scabbard. On ceremonial duty rather less practical accoutrements are required, including a kind of mayoral chain of silver metal, clasped by a gold crown, and secured to each shoulder by white satin bows. White lace ruffles at neck and wrist are worn with white gloves. Service medals on the chest, dangling from a colourful display of ribbons, are topped off with a badge round the neck; and, if possible, the star of an order of knighthood glints near the wearer's diaphragm.

Like Black Rod in the Lords, the Serjeant in the Commons also has a duty to maintain security, and for this reason the Sovereign has usually exercised an alternating choice between a high-ranking officer from the Army or Navy, and in modern times has added the Air Force as a third source of recruitment. After a time it was noticed that in the Commons, as distinct from the Lords, generals and admirals were still alternating without an air marshal to vary the order. A former Speaker's Secretary jokingly explained the deficiency as due to the inability of the RAF to produce a gentleman, a qualification considered essential for the post.

Meanwhile, complaints about dirt and neglect of the premises were difficult to justify when, in spite of war damage, standards were slowly rising above the low level of Edwardian days, when a Member wrote: 'We lime wash and disinfect cattle trucks and pigsties. Why cannot we poor Members be treated by the authorities as mercifully as our cattle?'

Although the three-fold tasks imposed on the Serjeant at Arms never struck the House as in any way inconsistent, his duties in fact appear as irreconcilable as would be those of Nureyev, were he required not only to dance impeccably costumed in the ballet *Swan Lake*, but at the same time to lower the safety curtain, keep intruders from the stage door and clean the auditorium before and after each performance.

It was something of a relief for the Committee to hear the uncomplicated story which Miss Doris Date told them on behalf of the waitresses. Upstairs in the Members' Tea Room, the female staff had no dressing room whatever, and had to change in the tiny service bars in the Tea Room itself. Downstairs the waitresses' dressing room was about fifteen feet square, containing nineteen chairs and a table, with twenty-six lockers and used by thirty waitresses. Not unexpectedly there had been continual complaints of overcrowding. Not only was the room itself deplorable, but also 'for psychological reasons they do not like to be down among the dirt, boilers and smell', declared the witness. The waiters too were having an uncomfortable time of it in their windowless and stuffy dressing room. Their spokesman made only a modest bid for improvement of their lot: 'We have one great need. There are two easy chairs and the rest have to sit on hard seats.' As for the women who served in the Tea Room, they had two breaks every day and should have somewhere to sit. 'They have not anywhere to go at present.'

'I think it is quite deplorable,' said the Chairman.

'It is terrible,' responded Miss Date, 'they have either to sit in the park or else go to the cinema.'

This evidence at least led to a firm recommendation by the Committee. Separate accommodation, suitably furnished for relaxation, was to be provided as a matter of urgency for male and female kitchen and refreshment room staff. For members, the best the Select Committee could do in the time available before the end of the session was to consider the possibility of providing more individual desks, if Members should require them. It was, therefore, recommended that a detailed inquiry, by means of a questionnaire to each Member, should be made to find out how many Members wished to have a permanent writing desk and how often this would be used. Richard Stokes's harvester was on its way. The result would not be known until the next session of Parliament in the following year. Meanwhile, the watchers at the edge of the field had already an inkling that the harvest would prove to be a lean one. One reason was the difficulty in which the Committee now found themselves. As the machinery of investigation ground on, they were at a loss to know what had been decided in the earlier part of their inquiry.

Men of affairs in business are accustomed to matters being agreed on the nod. Minute keeping is a comparatively recent innovation, and then only containing the brief record of an occasional board meeting, not a day-to-day note of operations. In the Commons, however, whatever has been decided has been formally recorded in a daily journal kept by the Clerk since November 1547. In that respect, Parliament has led the way. Its machinery is so efficient that there is never any occasion to dispute what has been decided – with the proviso, of course, that a decision has in fact been taken.

Mr Daines pointed out that in the course of a long and complicated inquiry, tentative decisions were often arrived at, without their being recorded in the minutes, but after a number of meetings in which some members of the Committee may not have been present, it was difficult to bear in mind and to recall those provisional decisions later. After a time doubts about the scope of their Clerk's activities led them to summon the Principal Clerk of Committees to explain what seemed a dereliction of duty. Mr L. A. Abraham proved to be a redoubtable witness and an expert in parliamentary law and procedure. The Committee asked him whether there was any reason why they could not have internal minutes, so that they would not be embarrassed by having a purely tentative decision entered on the formal minutes, which would in due course be published. Mr Abraham firmly advised them against any such expedient, 'You can enter anything on the minutes, but anything on the minutes will have to be reported to the House and published.' He described an instance of a Committee who made a decision to reject a proposal, which was duly entered on the minutes. Later the same Committee wished to reverse the decision. At that point the Committee came up against the rule that a negative decision cannot be rescinded. The Committee then went through a completely irregular process of purporting to rescind a negative decision. 'If you look at the minutes now you can see there, for the edification of posterity, the difficulty the Committee got into by committing themselves to a decision which they subsequently reversed. Generally, Committees, if I may say so respectfully, wisely avoid coming to a decision which they subsequently find themselves compelled to reverse when they have heard further evidence.'

The Stokes Committee still had to be taught the rudiments of efficient minute-keeping. The Chairman pleaded that perhaps the Clerk would make a note of items, just to remind the Committee at their next meeting.

'Yes,' replied the witness, 'I've had plenty of experience of that – it is a matter of extreme difficulty for the Clerk to know when things are decided on. What will probably happen . . . when these minutes are read at the next meeting, is that you have a long wrangle, Members saying "We did not decide that at all".' The trouble occurred whenever there were no rules of procedure. 'All I can say is, and I know the practice of the House as thoroughly as anybody, that I have never heard it suggested before that the Clerk should keep two sets of minutes, one the minutes of the proceedings and another the record of some other decisions. I cannot really conceive it. I do not know on what principle he would decide.'

The problem was finally resolved by the proposition that the Committee Clerk should keep a record of matters which the Chairman thought should be noted down for future reference, while the minutes of the Committee would follow strictly the practice of the House.

With one difficulty out of the way, the Committee met another. It was the attitude of some of the witnesses to this most serious problem of accommodation. They were not ready to accept the paramount interest of Members in the use of rooms in the Palace. While the Committee were working in units of yards and feet, and Members in terms of lockers, the Serjeant at Arms was thinking in terms of houses, not houses for Members but houses for himself and his staff.

'Why is it necessary,' asked Mr Stokes, 'that three Office Keepers should reside in the House, taking between them eleven rooms, three kitchens, three bathrooms and, in fact 2500 feet of superficial area?'

Once again the answer was that their presence was essential,

(*Top*) Star Chamber Court. One of Sir Charles Barry's eleven courtyards. Each court was designed to give light and air to spacious interiors, with a different aspect of spires, turrets or towers being visible from any standpoint below.

(*Bottom*) Star Chamber Court after infilling. A gracious glass-roofed colonnade, which Edward Barry had constructed as the Members' Entrance, was demolished to make way for this new building in Star Chamber Court which provided additional box-like rooms for Members.

(*Opposite*) A view of the carriageway which runs the whole length of the building, linking the Lords' courts with those of the Commons and designed to facilitate the movement of servants up and down a hundred discreet staircases.

(*Above*) Parliament and Bridge Street – an unresolved problem. Bridge Street to the right of the photograph is only 100 yards long. The Commons hoped it would form part of a pedestrian precinct round Parliament. The Greater London Council claim it is vital for traffic flowing between Westminster and South London across the Thames.

(*Above*) Commons Chamber
after the German air raid 1941.
Sir Charles Barry would have
seen in its destruction an
opportunity to build something
better. Sir Giles Gilbert Scott,
however, was hampered by
instructions 'to preserve all its
essential features'.

(*Opposite*) The Clock Tower
against a foreground of fire –
17 June 1974.
Not for the first time in the
history of Parliament, the
London Fire Brigade succeeded
in limiting the damage done
by a bomb explosion.

(*Top*) The new parliamentary annex. A model of the winning design for a new building, separated from Parliament by Bridge Street. The design was approved by a majority in the Commons in 1973, but cancelled in 1975 for reasons of economy.

(*Bottom*) This hut was built on a roof to provide room for additional Hansard staff. It blocked half the windows of the Commons Debating Chamber, designed by Sir Giles Gilbert Scott.

Members' underground car-park below Big Ben. Apart from objections on aesthetic grounds, the construction of the £2·5 million car park in New Palace Yard was opposed by the local authorities because it conflicted with their policy of reducing private traffic in central London.

(*Top*) The Victoria Tower from Big Ben. Parliament's roofs have three focal points, the Clock Tower (popularly known as Big Ben), the Victoria Tower at the far end over the Lords, and the central spire, which was Dr Reid's ventilating shaft.

(*Bottom*) New Palace Yard underground car park. On the left of the photograph, beyond William Rufus's 900-year-old yard, is the tower of St Margaret's, the House of Commons parish church. To the right, one of the famous catalpa trees leans precariously toward the entrance and exit of the Members' new car park.

'quite invaluable should anything go wrong at any time . . . if a Minister or anybody leaves an important despatch case behind and at three o'clock in the morning discovers his loss, the first person who is rung up is the Office Keeper, who is always on duty. It needs two to cover the twenty-four hours and a third in case of sickness.' But what about the houses?

The Deputy Serjeant had one. 'I do not think,' he told the Committee, 'that you would get anybody to take on the job without a residence. The attraction of the appointment to me was the house.'

Asked how many rooms there were in the 'rabbit warren', as the Chairman described 'that vast accommodation' of the Serjeant at Arms' own house within the building, his Deputy replied curtly, 'I do not know.'

The exact number of rooms remained a mystery, but they were believed to be forty. When later the Committee were shown over his house by the Serjeant himself, old Sir Charles Howard shocked them by remarking, 'Dammit, a feller has to live somewhere!' In his evidence, he was asked whether the residence could be cut down to more modest proportions, to contain for instance four bedrooms, two sitting rooms and the usual offices; he was prepared to accept the principle but added, 'I think you would have to go a bit bigger than that.'

After all their diligent taking of evidence the Committee found no solution of any broad character. At the end of another year they had got the answers to a questionnaire circulated to all Members. It implied a pathetically modest aim.

'Assuming that accommodation could be found for a pedestal desk to be made available for the exclusive use of individual Members, would you make substantial use of such a desk?'

About half the House, 295 Members, answered 'Yes.'

The report continued: 'Your Committee are convinced that a substantial number of Members would benefit from the provision of desks. The Minister of Works, however, is doubtful whether sufficient room accessible to the Chamber can be found for them.' A few yards away, on the principal floor, were the extensive residential premises of the Serjeant at Arms, in addition to his offices. It is a measure of the strength of tradition that a later proposal to move the residence to the top floor, and to allow Members to use the whole of the principal floor, was never seriously entertained.

Although the Stokes Committee, when they set out on their voyage of inquiry, were confident that they would discover drones in the hive, they were completely unable to penetrate the defences of the staff. One witness claimed he put in sixty to seventy hours a week, and when a member of the Committee, relying on an anonymous letter, challenged him and referred to his ownership of a city hat shop, he explained that he was only a director, not the managing director, of a small family millinery business employing ten girls, which detracted not at all from his long hours in the service of the House.

Others toiled through the night, saw dawn come up like thunder and generally worked themselves almost beyond human capacity. Nepotism was alleged, but again successfully refuted with a very modest table of relationships which demonstrated the linkage was only between two brothers and two pairs of sons following in father's footsteps at a lowly level of employment.

Prayers are still said in the House every afternoon. It could not be claimed that the four minutes that these take was a heavy burden, but even the Chaplain produced a ready response: 'The actual official duties of the Chaplain of the House of Commons cannot be described as arduous, though they include the inexorable necessity of attendance at a precise spot at an exact moment every day that the House is in session. . . . Moreover, every attendant within the walls, and they are many, has a claim upon his services and ministrations whenever or wherever they may be desired.'

The Stokes Committee did, however, succeed in seeing one important recommendation implemented. Expenditure in the Estimates for the maintenance of the buildings of the Houses of Parliament was, henceforward, to be shown separately from the cost of maintenance of other public buildings, in order to give the House a greater say in what was proposed to be spent. Up to 1967–8, this useful recommendation was followed. Since that session, the practice has been ignored by the Treasury and the annual cost of House of Parliament buildings cannot now be readily ascertained. Some published figures suggest it is in the region of £8 million or more a year, compared with £½ million when the figures were shown separately.

CHAPTER THIRTEEN

ROOM IN THE ATTICS

1960

Historians will perhaps look back on the 1960s as years of the greatest scientific advance since the beginning of the century, when space research was undertaken with remarkable energy. Stakes of 10000 to 1 were offered and accepted on the chance of a moon landing before the decade ended. At the time no man had made any flight whatever beyond the earth's atmosphere. By July 1969, Neil Armstrong, a civilian test pilot, after a training which began in September 1962, stepped down from the flying machine Eagle on to the surface of the moon.

It was also a period in which, after the failure of the Stokes Committee to eject the multitude of other users from the Palace of Westminster, followed by the death of Richard Stokes himself, Members of the Commons began to consider an almost revolutionary proposal: to find space for themselves outside the precincts of the Palace of Westminster. The very idea raised many constitutional questions, which have not yet been satisfactorily solved. What would be the position of Members in regard to parliamentary privilege? The serving of a writ upon a Member within the building had been ruled to constitute a serious breach of privilege. Would the law of Parliament protect them from such inflictions in an office over the street? The indications were that it would not, since the precincts only extended to a line midway down the centre of the roadway. This issue was raised by an interesting episode affecting a woman employed in the Commons kitchen after the war. A heavy suitcase she was carrying out of the building burst open, and tins of peaches and other foodstuffs much prized at that time rolled beyond the centre of the road. The police were ready to prosecute for theft, which they would not have been entitled to do without instructions from the House authorities if the mishap had occurred within the precincts.

The roof space scheme within the Palace was an immediate solution on a limited scale, but the debate of 31 March 1960 showed that a much more ambitious scheme would be needed if Members' demands were to be fully met. The Member for Bristol West, Mr Robert Cooke, regarded the expenditure of a quarter of a million pounds on the attics above the Committee Corridor as throwing money away. He urged the adoption of 'the great and grandiose scheme' by which Sir Charles Barry had proposed to complete the Palace by building round the courtyard from the Clock Tower along Bridge Street and then, after a corner gateway, to continue the building along the side of Parliament Square till it reached St Stephen's Entrance. This scheme, he claimed, would solve all problems of accommodation once and for all, with a minimum of disturbance to those within the Palace and none of the friction of trying to move them.

The Member pointed out that the building looked very unfinished in its present form, and begged Members to study the coloured prints in the Serjeant at Arms's office which revealed what was originally intended. These show what Barry had in mind. New Palace Yard is at present enclosed only by iron railings. When viewed from the higher ground of Bridge Street, the parliamentary buildings appear sunken and the sloping diagonal line of the ground diminishes their importance and impact. Accordingly, Barry planned to make Westminster Hall a grand centre enclosed by a range of buildings with an imposing gate-tower which he wanted to call the Albert Tower to correspond in some degree with the Royal Entrance below the Victoria Tower. Mr Cooke claimed that even the famous catalpa trees, which fringe New Palace Yard on the Bridge Street side, although old and dying could be moved and would survive.

The government declared that the Barry scheme would cost £5 million, and if only one wing were built instead of two, the cost would be over £1 million; they were opposed to it. Instead, the government proposed to acquire and develop a whole area bounded by Bridge Street, Whitehall, New Scotland Yard and the Embankment. The Minister of Works was considering 'rather long-term, but nevertheless, definite possibilities of building over Bridge Street', so that people who at present occupied rooms in the Palace but who need not be within the precincts to do their work, might move over there. Accommodation for use of the Commons, however, would only form a part of a complex of government offices.

Many Members were by no means satisfied with the government statement that measures to provide better accommodation for Members were 'under consideration'. The idea of a building over the road was described by Sir Peter Agnew as 'a somewhat visionary proposal' for those Members who had not got a great number of years before them in which they might hope to serve in the Commons. Sir Hamilton Kerr, agreeing with him, urged that they should concentrate on the short-term issue. 'Let us see what improvements we can effect within the existing limits of the Palace of Westminster, and let us see how the present system works.' He warned against one of the main difficulties for Members if they had to work in a nearby building – the harassment of Division bells. Unless they were in very good training indeed, 'I warn Members against the rush and helter-skelter of the Division bell from outside limits. The policemen, certainly those at the St Stephen's Entrance, are the most terrible sadists. Knowing that one has four minutes or more to spare, they say, "Hurry, Sir, you have only another half minute." I think they hope to see hon. Members really expire or being sick in St Stephen's Hall. I say that we are better situated if we are working inside the actual confines of the Palace.'

The honourable Anthony Wedgwood Benn (at that time the reluctant heir to his father's Labour peerage) put the opposite view. 'What we need is a new office block . . . there is a terrible danger that we shall look back all the time at the ancient traditions of Parliament and forget our modern requirements and allow ourselves to slip behind. I sometimes wonder,' he continued, 'at what stage the Beefeaters realized they were no longer men of war but were objects of curiosity to the tourist. What sort of man was the commander of the Beefeaters when this subtle change took place?' He would have been like the Minister of Works, concluded Mr Benn, advocating for good measure the nationalization of the Lord Great Chamberlain.

In any debate on the subject of Members' needs, there is usually a strong strain of resistance to change. Mr Michael Clark Hutchison, a Scottish Conservative, expressed his own views on the question of accommodation very plainly: 'I do not want any change whatever. In fact, I am delighted with the House and the Palace of Westminster. I have never found the accommodation too small or too overcrowded. There is always plenty of room in the Dining Room; the Smoking Room is adequate, the Library is very large and we are served very well by all the staff in those departments. All Ministers have rooms and there is plenty of space for Members on the lower floors and in the areas above the two Division Lobbies. I do not want a room for myself and I do not want a telephone. I detest that instrument enough already and I shall certainly take what steps I can to prevent one being foisted on me. . . . I like the House and its surroundings as they are.' It would, he said, be a mistake to think of the House as an office or business house and there was no reason to copy the American pattern or any other Parliament. Importing the first political comment into the debate, he added: 'In my view a lot of this "fussation" about accommodation is an agitation from those on the left wing. They want to put their fingers in the till and inflate themselves at public expense.'

A rather less controversial attack was made upon the system of control exerted by the Lord Great Chamberlain. Mrs Castle summed up the continuing frustration of Members in spite of the small changes achieved by the Stokes Committee. These improvements were very inadequate, she said. 'We can now have a cup of tea in the Tea Room without having it accompanied by the smell of kippers – that is something. We have had thirty-six more desks provided in six years. There is a new rest room for the kitchen staff. We have a new Lady Members' Retiring Room, which is nicknamed "Barbara's Castle", but what have we not got? We have not got fundamental improvements in the Library, or extensive building operations, not even a desk per Member, not even the 295 Members' requests for desks met. . . . Above all we have not got proper control over our own affairs which became the central demand of the Stokes Committee report.' She quoted the dictum (unconsciously ambiguous) of King George V when he opened the new County Hall, 'A public authority meanly housed is a public authority meanly esteemed.' The time had come, in Mrs Castle's view, for a House of Commons Commission to be in control of the whole building. The proposal was opposed by Mr R. A. Butler as Leader of the House, because it would be unthinkable and unworkable for the Commons to be put in charge of the Lords. He promised, however, in the terms of moderation of which he was a master, that the opinions of Opposition Members would be borne in mind. Indeed he went further and conceded a point to them. 'It may be,' he said, 'that the office of Lord Great Chamberlain is slightly anachronistic.'

There was no question in the government's mind, however, of removing from the Lord Great Chamberlain his ancient mandate. As for the beautiful catalpa trees, they would be condemned by the Barry scheme 'which we should all regret'. With the promise of future plans for new buildings in Bridge Street, the House showed itself, on a division, to be content to wait upon events.

CHAPTER FOURTEEN

A DIVAN IN THE BASEMENT

1963

The year 1963 was the penultimate of the thirteen years of Tory misrule, as described by Labour, when the country had never had it so good, in the opinion of the then Prime Minister, Harold Macmillan. It was a time of relative prosperity in the affairs of the nation, and on 1 August it seemed a moment in history when the private affairs of the comely Miss Christine Keeler, which had been so much in the public mind that summer, might be given a lower priority than the inadequacies of the building in which Members worked and its effect on their health.

The topic touched the responsibilities of several of Macmillan's most talented ministers. Enoch Powell was in the Cabinet as Minister of Health while Geoffrey Rippon was Minister of Public Building and Works. Lord Hailsham (who, thanks to the Peerage Act, was already looking forward to abandoning his peerage and re-entering the Lower House) was Lord President of the Council and Minister of Science, while R. A. Butler was Leader of the Commons.

The debate that took place revealed the manifold disadvantages of the building in that period. Mr Laurie Pavitt MP concentrated on the question of health: 'If an accident occurs . . . somebody has to get on the telephone and hope that the congestion of traffic will not prevent an ambulance being rushed from St Thomas's Hospital to render assistance.' The whole point of a health unit under a permanent medical officer, which he urged should be set up in the Palace of Westminster, was not merely to provide first aid. 'It would prevent people who are working hard from becoming ill. It would prevent hon. Members from suffering from the consequences of having to work for long hours with inadequate tools and facilities, and the stress and strain which is part and parcel of our job.' He asked the House to realize that it was no longer fevers but coronary thrombosis which has led to the deaths of Members in recent times. 'We all have sad memories of people of first-class calibre and intellect who made a great contribution in this House but who were taken from us and their lives terminated all too soon. This House bears a measure of responsibility for that,' he claimed, 'because of the work we do and the way in which we have to work. . . . We sit here lounging back on our green seats getting a crick in the neck, trying to keep an ear to the microphone and an eye on whoever is speaking on the benches opposite. I do not know whether Mr Speaker is more fortunate, but he sits in his Chair for longer hours than we do. Was advice taken from medical men about whether Mr Speaker's chair was right for posture? Do we have an occupational hazard merely because of the way in which the seats are built?' There was a clear need for relaxation, which Barry's building did not provide. 'At present,' he said, 'few Members could relax. In the Smoke Room, the Tea Room and in the corridors, we are all the time giving out nervous energy. We talk to our colleagues and to the Press. Most of us get here early in the morning and get home at midnight. During that time we burn up three times as much nervous energy as the average person.'

The uninitiated might be tempted to laugh, but the very vehemence of his pleading indicated the imperfections and the need for drastic change. The nineteenth century did not do business on the telephone. It was only considered a necessity in the twentieth. 'We met a gentleman from Hall's telephones whose company had actually installed one of the first machines in this place in 1908. . . . Whenever we try to conduct a conversation on the old-type telephones we feel we are plugged in to outer space or perhaps Jodrell Bank. All kinds of sounds and extraneous noises come over the telephone, but conversation is not at all clear.' Modern instruments, which should enable those Members who were a little hard of hearing to hear clearly the complaints of their constituents, were said by the Serjeant at Arms to be more than the House could afford, which, Mr Pavitt concluded, was ridiculous.

The conditions under which Members worked at this time were vividly described in a speech by Mr William Hamilton. When he first entered the House in 1950 he was given a key to a locker which was no bigger than the one he had had at school. It was the only accommodation which he had in the building. After twelve years' seniority, however, things had improved for him. 'I now have a little desk upstairs, right at the top. I go up in an old antiquated lift and I eventually get right to the top of the building. I am with another seven Members in a room the size of the average dining room in the average council house. All the time, every day in midsummer, we have to have artificial light. I sit furthest away from a very narrow window and I must put on the lights on an August day like today. The room is ideal for a suicide. If I could squeeze out of the window, I could throw myself, and sometimes feel like doing so, into the Thames. . . . The blunt fact is that this building was not built and is not equipped for a twentieth-century role.'

Mr Hamilton's conclusion was important and expressed the feelings of most of his colleagues. 'As an ordinary backbench Member, I have suffered over the years increasingly from the feelings of frustration, helplessness and impotence. Those feelings originate in large measure from the environment in which we work.'

He urged that a wholesale move should be made of Queen, Parliament, government departments and civil servants to a new administrative capital north of the Trent. It would be a Washington, a Canberra or a Berne, somewhere between York and Harrogate, linking the industrial north with the south, mid-way between Thames-side and Clyde-side. 'This is an enormously imaginative and bold project. It would undoubtedly present a tremendous challenge to architects, engineers, builders, town planners and others and it would strike a powerful and sorely needed blow at the idea that we in this country are hide-bound by tradition and conservatism through an undue reverence for everything that is old, musty and riddled with dry rot and wood worm.' There was only one factual error in Mr Hamilton's rejection of the old building. Barry's stone-work was mouldering but the interior woodwork after a hundred years showed not a single trace of wood worm or dry rot.

Another truth which emerged from the debate was that Members' business now involved the employment of secretaries, for whom again no allowance had been made in the old building, since the concept did not then exist that Members would find any need for a personal retainer, other than perhaps a footman, when they gathered within the walls of Parliament. As late as 1930, there were perhaps two typewriters in the entire House of Commons. The most literate of officials, the Clerk of the House, kept incoming letters, unfiled, in a black box, as his predecessors had done as far back as the Long Parliament of Charles I's reign. The Speaker's Secretary, Sir Ralph Verney, the last official to receive a baronetcy for his services in that capacity, made scant use of the pen. Answers to any letters were typed by the train-bearer, a former valet, and the letters themselves were usually either destroyed or returned to sender, decisions being retained in the memory alone. It was an age of considerable irresponsibility combined with meticulous observance of what was thought to be good form.

The King wore a brown bowler hat when he was completely off duty and not in Field Marshal's uniform, as he appeared on the boxes of King George mixture of Cadbury's chocolate. His concern for empire – the Empire – was demonstrated in his rebuke to his eldest son as a cad for wearing a cap – informal headgear known as a 'bounder'.

It was not until 1932 that the first solitary young woman typist, an almost anonymous Miss Smith, was engaged to work on the staff of the House of Commons. A year earlier, the first steel filing cabinet was introduced to hold the handful of letters which were kept from those days. It was already, however, a time in which the paper economies of the First World War had not been entirely overlooked. An order from the Stationery Office for one million adhesive labels, for re-use of old envelopes, was found among the dusty piles of paper in an office whose official output averaged half a dozen letters a week.

Thirty years later the entire picture had changed. The equipment of the ideal office which new Members expected to find was a private room containing a substantial desk, an individual telephone, a couch or day-bed for late night sittings, and, hovering in the background, a well manicured secretary, capable of producing forty of fifty letters a day. Such minimal office facilities were demanded but still not available at that date, although in foreign parliaments, notably in Washington, they were said to be commonplace. The Prime Minister, Harold Macmillan, told a Member who complained of conditions that the House of Commons was not a factory; but Members disagreed. 'One of the most appalling sights of the twentieth century is a battery of hens on a farm crammed in a confined space and forcibly fed,' declared Mr Pavitt. 'I think that the next most horrible sight is that of thirty-two secretaries crammed into inadequate accommodation in a manner which is unhygienic, unpleasant and probably unlawful.'

Sir James Duncan, a Conservative who fought hard for better staff conditions, interposed with the ambiguous assurance that 'We have tried to thin out the secretaries'. He pointed out that not all Members desired to do their work in the House. Many who were lawyers did all their constituency work in their offices in the Temple, and business men used the premises of their firms for their parliamentary work. 'There are others,' he continued, 'who are quite content to use the basement rooms and, as I do, to sit on a divan to dictate letters in the passage way.'

The informal advisory committee, of which Sir James was chairman, had recommended 'the fairly quick provision of a Parliamentary precinct on Bridge Street . . . and it should not be too long before every Member has the sort of accommodation that he thinks he needs'. Meanwhile, the attic rooms under the roof, which his committee had also recommended, were to be proceeded with immediatley during the summer recess, at a cost of half a million pounds. The difficulties of combining achievement with democracy, particularly in making any visible change in the neighbourhood of Parliament, was demonstrated in the ministerial reply. The advisory committee, in addition to the development of space under the roof within the Palace of Westminster, had recommended that an entirely new parliamentary building on the other side of Bridge Street should be provided as part of a general re-development of the Whitehall area, which included Scotland Yard, two undistinguished blocks of Victorian offices, and the eighteenth-century Richmond Terrace.

Sir William Holford, the leading town planner in England, and widely recognized abroad for his outstanding work in that field, had been asked to make a 'feasibility study'. The Minister, knowing the sensitivity of the House on such matters, was careful to disown any immediate intention of going forward on these proposals. 'His preliminary report is, I think we all agree, a valuable starting-point, but it does not represent a firm plan for the development of the site, let alone a design. Nor is it a blueprint for action by the government. I must emphasize that the government have not decided to carry out a particular scheme at any particular estimate of cost. We are not committed to any part of the scheme. We have received it, and we are considering it, and I hope that today's debate will enable me to get the sense of the House on the question. . . .'

Nobody could justly say that the Minister was being over-forceful, but his statement was too strong for Members. Mr Charles Pannell, destined himself to succeed as Minister of Public Building and Works within a year, looked askance at the appointment of 'the safe, the well-known and fashionable architects' and stressed the great care needed to see that the architectural profession produced its best. 'My appeal is that the Ministry of Works should take care to see that we get an inspired architect.'

What architect then should be chosen? Clearly not the past President of the Royal Institute of British Architects, who happened to be Sir William Holford. In Mr Pannell's view, what was needed was a map upon which a certain radius would be delineated, known as the precinct, and that everything within vision of the House should be within the control of Parliament. A Joint Parliamentary Commission with planning authority should then be set up 'to decide the sort of buildings of which this place should be the centre'. As for the type of building in the parliamentary precinct, 'it should match the present building – I do not mean that it should be Gothic – but it should be something more than Sir William has in mind. His plan seems to be nothing more than a shopping centre with a parliamentary annexe.' While the future Minister saw 'a noble vista with a widened Bridge Street to facilitate the flow of vehicles', Sir James Duncan was attracted by a shopping precinct away from the noise of traffic.

Richard Marsh, later to become Chairman of British Rail, regretted that Members had 'to spend long hours travelling backwards and forwards to cheap bedsitters' and urged that the new building might at least provide a room for Members who lived outside London. 'If I ran an organization,' he said, 'and found a member of my staff dictating letters on a bench in the foyer, I would kick him out, believing that that is not the way one works. It is certainly not the way a British Member of Parliament ought to work.'

The trouble was, however, as another Member revealed, that rooms alone are not enough. 'As the former Clerk of the House has now retired, perhaps I can relate what we found. He has to be here all the time the House is sitting and has to be available to Mr Speaker, sometimes urgently, for consultation. We found that he had a bedroom upstairs but had absolutely no method of cooking his breakfast except by one gas ring.' It was a sad picture on which the Speaker's Advisory Committee had stumbled during an early morning tour of inspection. Knocking on the door of what had been in more spacious days Erskine May's bedroom, when the Clerk had had a house overlooking Speaker's Court with twenty-six servants, they were surprised to find Sir Edward Fellowes crouched over a kettle endeavouring to make tea. It was a loss of dignity which Members felt should not be permitted. Accordingly, a part of the roof space was made into a decent flat for the Clerk, and within months a new Cabinet Minister, Mr Frank Cousins, used the former bedroom as his office, while Mr Denis Healey, the then Secretary of State for Defence, was accommodated in what had been Erskine May's dressing room. Ten years later, the Clerk's roof flat was again re-modelled to enable the Rev. Ian Paisley, the United Ulster Unionist Member from North Antrim, to occupy what had been the master bedroom.

The difficulty about all debates is that speeches are not enough in themselves, however brilliant or well delivered, to result in immediate action. All Members wanted something, even if it was only to leave well alone. The next step had to be based on practicality, on what the Minister could do or get away with not doing. Richard Marsh pointed out that Parliament was a place, first and foremost, in which it should be possible to operate effectively against the Executive; this was the vital need for backbenchers on both sides of the House. That fact, he claimed, was the real reason behind the lack of facilities so far. 'No Minister will dig his own grave by equipping people who might be awkward.' It was a clever analysis of the problem, but perhaps not an accurate one; it might be true to say that Ministers have always been timorous of their critics in the House and fear to move in any direction without a clear and compulsive mandate from Members of all parties. A demand for a squash court or gymnasium was put forward in the debate, but not strongly argued or supported, and any Minister who began to construct one would soon have fallen under fierce criticism. The only approach to unanimity was a desire that the Commons should be in charge of its own arrangements, and that meant getting release from the ancient control exercised by the Lord Great Chamberlain. If there was to be an overspill into Bridge Street, was the Lord Great Chamberlain, who still exercised the royal control of the Palace, to be there too? Such a position, said Mrs Barbara Castle, would be ridiculous: 'And that,' said the Minister in reply, 'is a matter that we shall want to consider very carefully.'

Sir James Duncan and his Advisory Committee had achieved something in bringing to the forefront of Ministers' minds both the needs of Members within the existing Palace of Westminster and proposals for new accommodation in a new building across the road. On 20 April 1964, Sir Leslie Martin, a brilliant designer of modern housing estates, university colleges and libraries, was appointed by the Minister, Mr Rippon, as consultant for the whole area at the bottom of Whitehall. His advice was required on the relationship of a new parliamentary building in Bridge Street to the present precincts of the Palace of Westminster, but his appointment was to be limited to consultancy. Architects would be appointed in due course to work within the consultant's general scheme, but Sir Leslie Martin would not be concerned with individual buildings.

There was soon to be a general election, bringing a new government to carry forward some or all of these plans. The government of 1964, the Labour Party manifesto promised, would give a lead with a probing review not only of the Departments of State but the work of Parliament itself. 'The dying months of a frustrating 1964 can be transformed into the launching platform for the New Britain of the late 1960s and early 1970s.'

CHAPTER FIFTEEN

THE BLACKSMITH'S FORGE

1964

Another year had gone by. The previous summer while Mrs Castle had been triumphing in debate over obtaining a ladies' retiring room near the Chamber, the first woman cosmonaut, Valentina Tereshkova, had made forty-eight orbits of the globe. Now in 1964 there was a new government in Britain, with Sir Alec Douglas Home as Prime Minister, and the Minister of Public Building and Works, Geoffrey Rippon, promoted to the Cabinet. At last there was hope of a real advance in the matter of accommodation. For the first time the government seemed ready to take the bit between its teeth, and break into a canter without waiting for the slowest-thinking among its supporters. One of them had written to *The Times*, 'Is there any need for an extension of the Palace of Westminster at all? Barry's building is huge and contains quite enough rooms for the use of our pampered, overpaid, overfed burgesses.'

The Speaker's Advisory Committee on accommodation had reported on 29 April that an extension should be built enclosing the third side of New Palace Yard to the north, and designed in the Gothic style. The Press had taken an interest in the proposal. Vehement and even virulent correspondence by partisans of the old and new had been published, evoking an argument, as it became known, between the Mods and the Goths. 'We have heard of the vandals, but who are these Goths?' asked an architect in a letter to the *Guardian*.

In a brilliant debate in the last summer before the general election, Mrs Castle's speech summarized the situation. She was an unrepentant protagonist for the plan, 'These Goths,' she said, 'are Members of Parliament who have succeeded in doing what no other Committee on accommodation has succeeded in doing in the past. We have stimulated widespread public interest and debate in the working conditions of MPs. . . .' Most of the initial outcry about the proposals had been about style. Style, she explained, was the least important of the recommendations. It was quite ancillary, following from other matters of principle. The proposal to build a new arm to the Palace of Westminster in Gothic style was only a way of highlighting the choice which Parliament had to make. As long ago as 1960, Hugh Gaitskell had defined that choice: 'Are we to go on tinkering with this problem, or should we really try to find a permanent solution?'

Tam Dalyell, within two years of entering the House as Member for West Lothian, had become so keen a student of the building's possibilities that he had personally located 140 rooms easily convertible for Members' use. There was a blacksmith's forge, historically linked no doubt with the mounting block in the courtyard for those who, like the Duke of Wellington, had trouble in reaching the stirrup unaided.

The Serjeant at Arms had given up most of his original house, but his residence still comprised seventeen rooms; why could he not live at St James's Palace? Once again the powers of the Lord Great Chamberlain were criticized, and not only on principle. 'Our charge,' complained Mr Dalyell, 'is that the Lord Great Chamberlain has failed to do the job he should do. That job is to exploit every nook and cranny in the Palace. Not 110 steps from the Bar of this House, I can show any hon. Member three completely unused dusty rooms. Down St Stephen's Hall, opposite a room used by the staff and up a staircase, there are three unused rooms which could easily become offices. Why is it that the Parade Room, with 690 square feet, is unused? I discovered there a man pressing his trousers. Is that right? Is it right that one of the most beautiful, elegant rooms in this Palace should be used for this purpose?'

Apart from the forge, he had found mammoth workshops and

woodwork rooms, which any architect with experience of converting slums could convert into rooms habitable enough for honourable Members. What of the rooms in the Lord Chancellor's private residence, which now numbered twenty-nine, or the twenty-four rooms which are occupied for his office, the rooms used by the Examiner of Private Bills, the Examiner of Local Acts, the Crown Office and the Judicial Committee of the House of Lords? 'We should serve an eviction order on all those who are not elected Members of Parliament,' concluded Mr Dalyell, 'with an expiry date on the fifth of November.'

Mr Wedgwood Benn placed the banderillos once more in the Lord Great Chamberlain's back. 'This question raises the whole point of the control of the Palace. Nearly 100 Members have joined me in tabling an Address to the Queen praying that control be taken away from the Lord Great Chamberlain. I have never met him. I believe him to be kind and cordial, but he is a grotesque anomaly and he has to be removed. If he did not exist, who would think of inventing him? If we planned to erect a building in Bridge Street, would somebody say, "Let us give it to a hereditary functionary so that he can run it for us?" 'This is fantastic.'

Nigel Birch, a former Minister of Works, objected to any addition to the Palace itself, since Barry's design already possessed the virtues of balance and symmetry. 'If we put an addition to the end of it,' he said, 'we are doing something barbarous. It is almost as if someone added a lavatory wing to the Parthenon and explained "It is quite all right, because we intend to build it in the Doric style."'

The debate ended in a general consensus that the existing Palace was a scandalous place in which to work, and that the need for additional accommodation was an urgent one. The government agreed to pursue the necessary technical and professional inquiries arising from the recommendations of the Advisory Committee, and after that to report back to the House. A general election, which they were due to lose, was just around the corner.

In the spring of 1965, the Lord Great Chamberlain's fief was at last brought to an end. Following advice by the Prime Minister to the Sovereign, the House of Commons became master in its own house in the fullest sense of the word. The control, use and occupation of the Palace of Westminster and its precincts was with the consent of the Queen removed from the Lord Great Chamberlain and vested in the Lord Chancellor and Speaker, each of them becoming responsible for the parts occupied by the Lords and Commons respectively. By this simple move, Members themselves became, for the first time in their long history, in charge of their own House. It was an earnest of the Labour Ministers' promise of a new way of life for the country. Their party manifesto had described the nature of their inheritance. 'Through their bankrupt and vacillating leadership, the Tory Government have bequeathed to Labour a Britain dragging its feet, side-stepping the challenging issues of our time, forced to linger temporarily in the wings of history.'

Two months later, on 22 June, both Houses of Parliament assembled in Westminster Hall to present Addresses to Her Majesty, in commemoration of Simon de Montfort's Parliament of 700 years previously. This solemn proceeding did not attract the public attention that might have been expected. It was not the first news story of the day and the evening papers only carried an account on the inside pages. Newly elected Members were deeply puzzled when the Queen, having entered Westminster Hall through St Stephen's Porch with a full fanfare of trumpets, was escorted to her chair of state not, as might have been anticipated, by the Lord Chancellor and Speaker but by the Lord Great Chamberlain and the Minister of Public Building and Works. Despite the solemn assumption of authority in their own House two months earlier, the Commons of England had not in fact established their full rights, and the old dispute over the custody of the Great Hall of Westminster was still being carried on under the very nose of the Sovereign.

The separation of the two Houses and their individual responsibilities under their respective presiding officers led to unforeseen difficulties. What had been clear before was that overall control was exercised by one personage, somebody, albeit absent most of the time, who could be identified and blamed. When, for example, Mr Gooch, a Norfolk trade union Member representing agricultural workers, had his cupboard broken open and his typewriter stolen, Mr Speaker Morrison disclaimed responsibility because the theft happened at the the weekend, when the Lord Great Chamberlain was in charge. Under the new rules, an imaginary line was assumed to be drawn across the Central Lobby, and what happened on one side was of no concern to the other House. Custodians who assisted the police in security patrols could no longer claim that their orders were from the Lord Great Chamberlain. They were now commanded from Lambeth Bridge House, under the Ministry of Works. When they left their office in the Lords, the crossing of the imaginary line brought the custodians under the operational orders of the Commons Serjeant at Arms. The Inspector of Police had his office in the Commons. His constables, on crossing the line towards the Lords, came notionally under the orders of Black Rod and the authority of the Lord Chancellor.

In St Stephen's Hall, the Serjeant at Arms was in control under the Speaker's authority. Below stairs, in the Crypt Chapel, the Lord Great Chamberlain still lurked, laying the law down jointly with the Lord Chancellor and Speaker. The solemnization of matrimony, for example, was not allowed in the Crypt Chapel for Commons staff below the highest grade, not from any rule of the Church but by edict of long standing by the Lord Great Chamberlain and his coadjutors. Again, at the Opening of Parliament, Members' wives could only be admitted to the ceremony with tickets issued by the Lord Great Chamberlain.

The Speaker of the Commons sought advice on the many points at issue from a new Select Committee on House of Commons Services. Increasingly through the years which followed, this Committee became more and more the effective power in the administration of the House, and the Speaker's former authority in the administrative field was correspondingly diminished. It was now the Services Committee to whom the House officials turned for guidance and to whom they made their reports. The Speaker held aloof as a kind of constitutional monarch, to be advised when the Services Committee deemed it useful to do so. The Committee took many minor decisions in the name of the Commons, only reserving the major ones for the House itself to decide.

CHAPTER SIXTEEN

A HUT ON THE ROOF

1967

On 27 July 1967 the House of Commons Services Committee, with Mr Richard Crossman in the Chair, made a report containing plans in outline for the erection of a new building round New Palace Yard, chiefly for accommodation of Members, with another building on the far side of Bridge Street for offices. The Services Committee regarded the recommendations for planning the long overdue essential accommodation 'worthy of serious consideration' by the House. Since, however, the proposal to build round New Palace Yard raised 'issues of taste which could override arguments of convenience', the Committee thought the House would like to debate the proposals before detailed plans were prepared. It was a half-hearted endorsement which almost suggested that the House would not desire to entertain any more hare-brained ideas.

Yet on the same day the Committee resolved on the motion of a Conservative, Sir Gerald Wills, without even reporting their resolution to the House, that 'additional accommodation for Hansard staff be provided by building a hut on the roof outside the East Gallery to the Chamber'. The result of this extraordinary decision – with the subsequent addition of a second storey to the hut as recommended by the Services Committee in November 1970 – has been to black out, with a cheap wooden structure of the type used by the Army when permanent buildings are impracticable, the whole range

of windows down one side of the Commons Debating Chamber, as
well as hiding its graceful exterior stonework.

Perhaps the best of Sir Giles Gilbert Scott's changes in designing
the new Chamber was to insert, in place of the stained glass of the
old House, wider clear glass windows through which Members in
the Chamber below could catch glimpses of sky or passing clouds,
and which on bright days avoided the need for artificial light. The
two decisions of the Services Committee, first for a one-storey and
then for a two-storey hut, resulted in what can fairly be described as
a piece of insensitive vandalism. Because it was done quietly and in
two stages, the change was accomplished without comment or
criticism by the House.

Members were, however, concerned at the time over another
decision by the Committee which was reported to the House and
which referred to an experimental change in the writing paper and
envelopes used by Members. The crests on the stationery at that
time were the royal arms in either blue or red, to indicate party
allegiance, or embossed in white with the address in black Gothic
lettering. The question has always been taken very seriously. On
one occasion the Librarian was held to be showing party prejudice
because the Library attendants unwittingly distributed in the letter
racks too many sheets of notepaper and envelopes of one colour and
not enough of the other.

It was now proposed to replace all colours with green, a traditional House of Commons colour, supposedly favoured by Henry
Tudor, the last Monarch to live in the Palace. The report continued:
'Your Committee are, however, reluctant to propose such a drastic
change without Members being able to express their opinions.'

Another daring innovation was to substitute the Westminster
portcullis for the royal coat of arms, which had been in general use
in the public service.

Meanwhile the idea of a Bridge Street development had been
most carefully examined by a Sub-Committee of the Services
Committee and the main difficulty for the planners pointed out – the
need to cross Bridge Street with its constant flow of traffic. The
Sub-Committee were told by the Ministry of Public Building and
Works that there was no prospect of Bridge Street being closed to

vehicular traffic for many years, if ever. Bridge Street was regarded not only as a physical barrier but also a psychological one. However ingenious the proposals for linkage, Members would not wish to be so isolated from the centre of parliamentary life, namely the Chamber. The Sub-Committee were therefore unanimous in their view that putting up a large parliamentary building on the other side of Bridge Street was founded on a false premise. Members certainly required more accommodation, but it should be near the Chamber. The proposed building might well prove a waste of money. Even at that time there were some rooms available at No. 1 Bridge Street, but it was difficult to find Members willing to occupy them. The more the Sub-Committee studied the project, the more they were convinced that it was impracticable. The proposed new building was intended not only to meet present needs, but to fulfil the needs of Parliament for many years to come. It was vital for the plan to be right and not a poor compromise. The Sub-Committee therefore considered two alternative suggestions. The first, which they dismissed as impracticable, was for the offices and residences of the House of Lords to be put in a new building in Black Rod's garden, below the Victoria Tower, so that the Commons could move into the accommodation thus vacated. It was virtually what Sir John Wardlaw-Milne put forward more than twenty years before.

The second suggestion, which the Sub-Committee favoured, was the completion of the original Barry plan by building round New Palace Yard, combined with limited in-filling on the site of the present Palace. The catalpa trees, whose existence seemed to have frustrated the Barry scheme on several previous occasions, were now alleged to have only a few more years of life, and could be removed. The new L-shaped building would be lower in height than Barry's, in order to preserve the view of the finials and skyline of the main building. No attempt would be made to copy the Gothic architecture of the Palace, but the new architecture would have a perpendicular character in sympathy with the existing building. This would be a building capable of providing rooms for at least 400 Members, with additional conference and secretarial space, at a cost of £1850000.

The proposal was calculated not to harm any of the main features of the Palace or the balance with Westminster Abbey opposite. The Sub-Committee thought that the whole scheme could be happily rounded off by building an underground car park – at a cost of £250000 – beneath New Palace Yard, as parking in the enclosed yard would seriously detract from the aesthetic appearance of the new building. Another and less happy idea of the Sub-Committee was that a building should also be erected in Commons Court, over the Members' Tea Room, involving further in-filling within the courtyard.

On 9 April 1968 Mr Fred Peart took over responsibility from Richard Crossman as Chairman of the Services Committee. Their report to the House on that day contained several important recommendations. The Committee were 'strongly of the opinion that any further in-filling in the existing Palace is undesirable'. It was a key recommendation and a welcome embodiment of common sense, representing a last chance to save the Palace from a return to the undignified huddle which the fire of 1834 and Barry's generous designs had cleared away. Unhappily, however, the good sense of the previous session on the disadvantage of a parliamentary annex on the far side of the traffic-laden Bridge Street was now completely contradicted. The excellent scheme of providing 500 rooms in a new building round New Palace Yard, on a modified line of Barry's original idea, had been illustrated with photographic models, showing a daylight scene and a night-time perspective. It was too dramatic for some Members to be shown what was to be done. They could not tolerate the replacement of railings and the removal of the West Indian catalpa trees, with the trumpet-shaped flowers which were so seldom seen in bloom.

'Many representations were received objecting to this proposal,' reported the Committee sombrely. It was all so different from Barry's approach; he would cheerfully have raised the roof of Westminster Hall to give that barn-like structure better proportions, had he been given his way.

The Minister of Public Building and Works put forward an alternative, which he did not personally recommend, but which would have solved all problems at a stroke. It was a proposal to forget all the tinkering and in-filling of the courtyards of Barry's masterpiece, the box-like windowless rooms under the roof, the blacking out of windows, and to construct a new House of Commons on the site between Bridge Street and Richmond Terrace. The probable cost would be £20–25 million, and the time taken would be fifteen to twenty years.

The Committee had no hesitation in rejecting this plan, preferring instead to reconsider the idea against which they had so firmly pronounced a few months earlier as being 'founded on a false premise' and which 'might well prove a waste of money'.

A revised plan for a Bridge Street building was put forward by Sir Leslie Martin as adviser to the Minister on the redevelopment of the whole Whitehall area. If Members could not get over the street, then let it be raised to enable them to get under it.

Barry's objection to the sunken appearance of the existing parliamentary buildings when viewed from across New Palace Yard was forgotten in a plethora of new ideas provoked by this happy scheme of a higher street level. There would now be room for a spacious entrance hall underneath the raised street, leading directly to a new building running the whole length of Bridge Street, which would then become part of the precincts of the Palace. Edward Barry's colonnade could be reconstructed to bring Members along a high-level walk above it on the east side of New Palace Yard and so directly to the Chamber without the need of lifts. The entrance to the underground railway in Bridge Street, together with the row of useful shops, would disappear, but at the back of the new Parliament building would be new government offices running all the way to Richmond Terrace, opposite Downing Street.

The Committee were told that the total cost, including the new building with entrance hall under Bridge Street, raising street level and building the special access to the Chamber along the colonnade would be around £5 million; it could be completed in six years. The new building would not, of course, replace the House of Commons or its Debating Chamber. It would only provide individual rooms for Members and their secretaries, and some of the administrative offices of the House.

The question of the car parking was considered. Unfortunately, space for car parking could not be provided under the new building, for the underground railway was there already. It would, however, be possible to provide a car park underneath New Palace Yard at an additional cost of £250 000 and this the Committee recommended.

The main difficulty in extending Parliament in this crowded area has always been the traffic in Bridge Street. An immense amount of traffic comes over Westminster Bridge from the east, using Bridge Street on the route westward; and more traffic comes from central London down Whitehall, turns left through Bridge Street and thence eastward over Westminster Bridge. The solution would be to build tunnels, and the Committee recommended that the planning of these should aim at the eventual stage-by-stage completion of a parliamentary precinct.

It was a very long term plan, on the attainment of which the Ministry of Transport and Greater London Council gave the Committee very little hope. The car park plan also seemed to go against ridding the parliamentary precinct of traffic. The Committee, however, ended their report with the optimistic reminder that 'the sooner a decision can be reached, the sooner can plans be put in hand and the building begun'.

Action was in the air at last. For better or worse there was to be a new building on the far side of Bridge Street, and the old frustrations of Members dictating in corridors would finally be resolved. Some time earlier the government had announced that a competition limited to Commonwealth architects would be held for any new parliamentary building. Accordingly, in January 1969, a mere nine months after the report of the Services Committee, assessors were announced for the competition. The House was fortunate in enlisting four most distinguished professional men as judges of the best design entered. They were Sir Robert Matthew, Mr Eric Bedford, Mr Denys Lasdun and, from Canada, Mr John C. Parkin.

Events were now moving fast, and the Services Committee felt able to turn their attention once more to the vexed question of stationery. Every Member had been circulated and some 400 replies received. Of these about half wanted to retain the quarto size paper which the Services Committee had thought of abandoning, as its use had been discontinued throughout the public service. In view of the large demand for it, however, the Services Committee were reluctant to recommend its discontinuance. The blue and red crested paper, which it had been hoped to drop, would be continued, and in addition quarto paper in this style should be available to Members on demand from the Serjeant at Arms's stores. The experimental green portcullis badge paper should be generally distributed and on permanent supply throughout the Commons. 'The badge and address should be embossed slightly lower down the paper and the telephone number removed. The badge on the flap of the matching envelopes should be embossed, not printed as at present, and the address removed. The embossed crest on the present plain white and flimsy paper should be replaced by an embossed portcullis badge.'

The interest of the Services Committee in the minutiae of stationery supplies was remarkable for one small breach with tradition. The white paper containing a black address in Gothic lettering was no longer to be supplied.

The Services Committee had, however, to report to the House a disturbing set-back to their hopes for the new parliamentary building. The responsible Ministers had confirmed that the ultimate objective was the closing of Bridge Street to traffic. Now it appeared that plans for tunnels to divert traffic would be extremely difficult and costly. The Greater London Council had told the government that far from reducing the flow of traffic along Bridge Street, the traffic authority was asking for the new building to be set back twenty feet to allow, if necessary, for the widening of the roadway.

The GLC also called to mind their responsibility for the development of amenities for the whole area; there was no question of using rate-payers' money to stem the traffic through Bridge Street. The implication was that GLC members valued the amenity of driving hell for leather past Parliament on their way to County Hall across the river.

The Minister of Public Building and Works therefore asked that the architectural competition should proceed on the understanding that it would not be possible to remove the traffic and that the building line should be set back twenty feet.

The Services Committee were dismayed. Their recommendation for the new parliamentary building on the far side of Bridge Street had been made because they had been informed that in due time it would be possible to divert all traffic and to create a parliamentary precinct as envisaged in Sir Leslie Martin's plan for the Whitehall area. They were now being asked to decide about the new building without any guarantee that traffic could be removed. The need to get ahead with the building was, however, paramount. It was now March 1970 and Members could not perform their duties efficiently without additional rooms. The Committee therefore reluctantly confirmed their earlier recommendation that the building competition should go forward, after the competitors had been informed of the new and unexpected restrictions.

In July the competition was launched, and by December 1970 nearly 1000 applications had been received, some 300 being from overseas; 246 entries were eventually put in. It was to be two years before the results were announced. The idea of a competition was fair enough in theory: youth might have a greater ability than age, and all should have a chance, but it went against the mature experience of the government department concerned. None of the leading names in British architecture submitted designs. The Services Committee thought that this was strange, and wondered whether there were some underlying reason. They should not have had to look far. In most professions established skills are available and known. Services can be obtained on payment of the appropriate fee, and the work done. It was on this principle that the House decided, on the advice of Lord Winterton's Rebuilding Committee, to enlist Sir Giles Gilbert Scott. His design followed the instructions of his employers. They got what they wanted, and there was no serious delay. A competition is not likely to attract established architects. Few would care to enter the lists against a thousand newcomers, and although brilliance may come to light through a competition, controversy follows, as it did in Barry's case, as night follows day. The delays caused by the open competition in 1970 finally resulted in nothing being built, which was surely not foreseen or intended at the time.

The alternative to the competitive process was demonstrated in the case of the underground car park. However monstrous this project was later thought to be, it was undertaken and brought to a relatively speedy completion in the form which the Services Committee had decided, although at a cost ten times greater than the original estimate for 200 cars given to the Services Committee in 1967.

In June 1971 the Services Committee, with Mr William Whitelaw in the chair, approved the plan for an underground car park with places for 500 cars. The scheme, they declared, would not only avoid detracting from the architectural merit of the Palace, but would result in 'a great aesthetic and amenity gain'. Parking on the surface would be banned except perhaps on occasions 'such as a big division at ten o'clock'. Instead of a courtyard filled with cars, there would be a grass centre, suitably landscaped, with a roadway round it, so that cars would circle clockwise on a one-way system leading in and out of the car park beneath.

When the report advocating the scheme came up in the House in the following month, it evoked no discussion whatever. Mr Whitelaw was ready to explain the Committee's decision but, as no Member questioned it, the report was approved 'on the nod' without a word spoken.

The construction of the car park involved the employment of a substantial number of Irish labourers, and the House authorities found it difficult to distinguish between a labourer arriving with a bag of cement and a man arriving with a pack of gelignite. The latter caused very substantial damage to the building on the west side of Westminster Hall when it was maliciously exploded.

Members had already become aware of the cranes, the bulldozers, the drills, the industrial strikes, the yellow-helmeted Irish navvies, the builders' huts and the diver who went down at night to plumb the waters. They were indignant, and claimed that the report had been rushed through at short notice. It was, in fact, approved at 11.07 a.m., three minutes after the start of a Friday morning sitting.

Houses, statues, towers and bridges strike the eye, and critics are usually alert to condemn them at a very early stage in their planning. An underground car park, however, remains invisible and opposition in the House did not become vocal until it was too late to do anything but denounce what seemed the senseless tearing-up of New Palace Yard, at great expense, for a five-storey underground building which has remained largely unused.

Meanwhile, the need for extra accommodation for Members was being urged on the members of the Services Committee. There had been a change of government since the Select Committee of 1968–9 had recommended building an extra storey on top of the Tea Room in Commons Court. The Services Committee now sought to meet Members' demands for more accommodation by providing a building of three storeys with forty-nine additional rooms. Without any overt pronouncement of a change in policy, it began to be felt that a room for each Member must be a standard to aim at. The only disadvantage mentioned by the Committee was that the proposed building would block out the windows in the Committee corridor.

Fresh from blocking half of Sir Giles Gilbert Scott's windows in the Debating Chamber, they could hardly have appreciated that this was a major blow at one of the great features of Barry's Palace. There was a 200-yard-long corridor on the first floor, all the windows of which faced west or south, above the river front which the Committee rooms overlooked. The corridor was built on a plan which Pugin had successfully included on a small scale in a country house. The effect was striking, and what has been destroyed through the imperception of the Services Committee was accurately recorded by a visiting reporter in the 1840s: 'Innumerable gleams of light cross the floor from one side, and reveal continuous ranges of windows. Bar-like shadows alternate with these gleams; the two give a peculiarly interesting effect to the far sweep of the vista. The warm, rich colour of the wainscot, their carvings and those on the lofty doors, with benches inset in slight recesses, makes a novel and magnificent whole. There is nothing to match its proportions anywhere in England.'

The Royal Fine Art Commission was adamant, when the plan was made to build the attics in the roof space, that no windows should be made in the Palace roof. They must have been unaware, or asleep, when the windows down one side of the Debating Chamber and the windows in Barry's magnificent corridor were heedlessly blacked out.

CHAPTER SEVENTEEN

A WINNING DESIGN AGAIN

1972

In March 1972 the four architectural assessors reached their decision, and Mr Julian Amery, as Minister for Housing and Construction, announced the successes in the competition. The authors of the winning design were two London architects in their early thirties, Robin Spence, a nephew of Sir Basil Spence, and Robin Webster, who shared the tax-free £8000 prize. The second prize of £4500 went to other London architects, and the third, of £2000 each, went to a British architect in San Francisco and two in Edinburgh.

The main feature of the winning entry was a covered open space at ground level, the size of Leicester Square, which would act as a focus for tourists and citizens. Reared over their heads, on four 'feet' at the corners, was a mighty rectangular block clad in bronze and glass, 100 feet high, hanging clear of the ground from a roof grid of steel. The new building was to offer Members a standard of accommodation and amenity undreamt of across the road. On the roof terrace there was to be a 'secret garden', but the public below would be able to look up and see Members at work, and a combination of fast lifts and a travelator under Bridge Street would bring them swiftly in to vote whenever the division bells rang.

From fellow architects there was a warm and generous welcome for the young men's victory, but experienced and therefore cynical civil servants were already predicting that Members, whom the

Minister announced were to be 'sovereign in this matter', would 'never wear' the daring design of the new parliamentary annex. Already the press officers were tending to overdo it. 'The offices for MPs are generous, well-proportioned rooms giving magnificent views. . . . Carrels for the MPs' secretaries are in wide landscaped galleries, with a view down to the covered urban square.' Apart from observing MPs at a distance, in the galleries above their heads, the public would also be entertained by watching large television screens and newscasters which would act as an extension of the public gallery of the Commons, 'and can also link our capital city and parliament with other cities and parliaments in Europe and the world'. In case of riot or civil disturbance as a result perhaps of things they might see or hear, a grille would drop like a modern portcullis between the four feet of the giant, enclosing or shutting out the citizens.

It was two years since the Services Committee had recommended to the House that there should be a competition. The competition had been held and the four distinguished architects had made their decision unanimously in reporting on the winning design: 'This is a solution of outstanding merit.' That stage might have been taken as the start of building. Parliament, however, has never worked as fast as that except in time of war, when thirteen bills passed through all stages in both Houses and received the Royal Assent in one brief afternoon. The programme for the new building required a reference back first to the Services Committee and subsequently to the House itself. The intention of the two young architects was to give the public, and not the parliamentarians alone, some benefit, and it was now the turn of those who represented the public to have their say. First, however, the two Robins were subjected to quite a fierce examination by the Committee itself.

'You said that none of the windows open. Does that include the roof?' asked a Member.

'In the summer,' replied Robin Webster, 'the roof can be wide open to allow the podium [a raised and covered platform open on all sides] to be without a top.'

'No,' retorted his questioner, 'I am asking about the roof garden you have constructed in the top of the building. There are a lot of plants there. Plants and people have different habits. Have you allowed for that? Can you explain how Members are going to enjoy being at the top with all the plants?'

Mr Webster was a little nettled. 'We shall choose plants to put up at the top which would be adapted to the English climate. We are not envisaging a tropical garden. I would just add that the climate up at the top is not the same as the climate in the offices. It is more an outdoor climate.'

Another Member regretted the ignorance of the competitors about the lives led by Members of Parliament. Most Members, he pointed out, like to be near the Chamber, and, therefore, lobbying went on as close to the Chamber as possible. It was unlikely in those circumstances that Members would walk some distance underneath Bridge Street, go up in a lift and then use the roof garden. They would be more inclined, if they could spare the time, to go to their club for lunch, or even take a walk along the river. Therefore, he felt that, attractive though it was, and however good a top to the building a roof garden might make, it was a rather elaborate provision of leisure for Members of Parliament.

The inquisition by the Committee was followed by faint praise from the Royal Fine Art Commission. What a pity, they said, that this imaginative scheme, which was clearly the best solution and which deserved to be carried to completion, should not have been that little bit better. 'The building is self-isolating and impassive, designed to be seen four-square. Its form and finishes are sober, smooth and uncompromising. These qualities contribute to, but also make demands upon, the immediate surroundings. . . . The treatment of the whole area in this idiom could be disastrous.' The new building was rather too high and should be lowered. The Commission, whose number included Sir Hugh Casson and Mr John Piper, agreed that it was a good idea to encourage the public to use 'this imaginatively provided open space', but at street level there should be souvenir shops, cafés, newspaper kiosks and the like. 'The building has an exciting and novel structural system which to the Commission's regret is not clearly expressed externally. The elevations, in their view, should illustrate, indeed underline, the drama of the fact that the building does not support but is suspended from the roof.' What is the good of structural daring, they asked, if the block looks 'over-bland and uncommunicative'?

The Westminster City Council was more definite than the Fine Art Commission in its insistence that the design of the building should not be considered in isolation but in a carefully planned relationship with the other surrounding buildings, both old and new. The original square block of New Scotland Yard by Norman Shaw, the later Victorian architect, must be preserved. Then there were the shops in Bridge Street to consider. It was essential that these should be replaced on a satisfactory pedestrian route between Whitehall and the Victoria Embankment. The shops were used by millions of tourists, as well as by civil servants and other workers, Members of Parliament and visitors to the Houses of Parliament. The building would interfere with the movement of pedestrians. There was a need to preserve the subway and make better provision for the loading and unloading of goods vehicles.

Under the plan, the direct access to the underground station from Bridge Street was to be cut off. In view of the heavy interchange of bus and underground passengers in Bridge Street, it was very important to maintain direct access to the station at that point and not, as proposed, somewhere else around the corner. So much for the local objections from the City of Westminster. The criticisms by the Greater London Council dealt more widely with the whole setting in which the building was to be put up. The tone of their memorandum was a good deal sharper.

The GLC were interested in widening both the pavement and carriageway of Bridge Street, and the Services Committee agreed generally with their evidence. In spite of the Council's clearly expressed views and the recommendation of the Services Committee, provision for this had not been made a condition in the architectural competition for the new Parliament building. The Department of the Environment explained, in answer to protests, that the assessors had wanted to keep the new building in line with the Treasury Building across the way at the far corner of Whitehall. This building line, which the Department of Environment itself favoured, would have resulted in no widening of Bridge Street at the Embankment corner and only ten feet more width at the corner of Parliament

Street. This would have meant virtually no more worthwhile space either for pedestrians, which the Services Committee desired, or for traffic. The GLC confirmed its decision as the Highway Authority that the wider road was necessary, and asked for twenty feet throughout its length to permit the addition of a bus lane together with a widened pavement.

Its Planning Committee objected most forcibly to piecemeal planning of one building at a time, which was apparently to be substituted by Parliament for Sir Leslie Martin's plan of unified development of the whole area. The GLC had expressed reservations to that plan at the time, but an overall concept was essential. This was not being done, and gave the GLC grave cause for concern. Parliament had already permitted the great blocks of government offices in Horseferry Road to diminish the scale of the Houses of Parliament when viewed against the wider scene of featureless office slabs. The new building in Bridge Street, if proceeded with, would further detract from Parliament's setting and make it a subordinate rather than a dominant feature in the immediate neighbourhood of Bridge Street and the Embankment.

Mr Robson-Smith, the Chief Planning Architect, pointed out that the two Robins, instead of keeping to the required height of 80 feet, had raised it, through the addition of the roof garden, to 105 feet. The omission of one storey would have made the plan to that extent more acceptable. On height, on relationship to other buildings, the GLC was flatly opposed to the plan.

There was now a new chairman of the Services Committee and Leader of the House, Mr Robert Carr.

'Do you believe,' he asked, 'this is an asset to the area, or is there a danger that a modern building like this might develop into a monstrosity such as you have allowed to happen on the other side of the river?'

The GLC witness was ready with his retort. 'As a matter of fact, we did object to St Thomas's hospital.'

The Services Committee disregarded all the major objections by the GLC but recommended that the House should adopt the winning design with a few modifications. The height could be dropped, but only by five feet. The bronze colour might not be quite appropriate and a rather lighter colour might fit in better with the surrounding and recently cleaned buildings. More security and some shops at ground level would seem desirable. The Committee were not, however, unanimous; eleven Members voted for and three against Mr Robert Carr's draft report.

CHAPTER EIGHTEEN

THE GREAT
OPPORTUNITY

1973

In March 1973 the Conservative Chancellor of the Exchequer (Mr Anthony Barber), had just introduced his budget outlining his attack on inflation, which had reached the alarming figure of 10 per cent. Things began to resemble the situation of the 1840s all over again, not of course that they were hungry years yet, but because any emphasis on Members' comforts and luxurious surroundings was irksome to their constituents, who after all had to put up the money. The longer the delay in pushing to its conclusion the exciting plan by the two Robins, the slighter would be the chances of bringing it to fruition.

At the end of the budget week, Mr Patrick Cormack, a Conservative Private Member, urged in a motion before the House that the new parliamentary building 'be not proceeded with'. It was a direct challenge to the whole elaborate design. He did not deny the need for better accommodation for Members and their secretaries. 'The picture of Members crammed eight to twelve to a room, dictating to secretaries on odd benches and in corridors was,' he said, 'a familiar and largely accurate one.' There were only ten rooms which Members could book on the interview floor below the Chamber, in which to speak privately with their constituents, and these rooms were in such great demand that it was sometimes necessary to book a month in advance. The case for the new building over the road rested solely on the acknowledged need for more accommodation. Why, he asked, could not the extra rooms be found in existing buildings in the neighbourhood? He saw danger in the proposed new building, which was still at the preliminary sketch plan stage, since it was going to offer far more than rooms for Members. There were going to be sauna baths, massage rooms, a television studio, a swimming pool and a roof garden. There was all the difference in the world between having an office across the road and the equivalent of the Inn on the Park Hotel. Above all, he was concerned about the effect on Members themselves. 'I think that we should beware of creating a new creature out of a natural desire to supply extra creature comforts for the old,' he warned. Before they embarked on a process of turning their backs on the old system, it should be remembered that Members of Parliament were not immune from the laws of nature and of man, and that work expands to fill the space available. To provide more rooms in existing accommodation within or just outside the Palace would cost some £2 million, but this sum would pale into insignificance against the cost of the new building designed by Robin Spence and Robin Webster. Members of Parliament were traditionally supposed to keep a wary eye on the nation's purse, but if they went ahead with the new building they would not be keeping the purse. They would be snatching the bag.

Mr Charles Pannell strongly disagreed with Mr Cormack. He begged the House not to cast aside the opportunity to create a noble parliamentary building, reminding them that he had been responsible, as Minister of Works, for the only new building in the Palace for over 100 years – the Star Court building.

The Minister for Housing and Construction (Mr Paul Channon) disappointed the supporters of the scheme by giving a judiciously neutral reply, not committing himself beyond his personal hope that there would not be any more in-filling of Barry's courtyards, since that would create a tunnel effect in the minor courts and great inconvenience during the building work. The total cost of the competition-winning building would now, he explained, be much higher than the £5.4 million of the original estimate. First, demolition of existing buildings and the uncertain climate of tendering would suggest that £10.5 million could well turn out to be on the low side. Then, strengthening the underground railway, moving the ticket office and entrance, and the reprovision of Cannon Row Police Station, would cost perhaps £9 million. Thirdly, the cost of land, professional fees and furniture would come to between £9 and £10 million. The whole project would thus amount to £30 million, but if the House were prepared to use existing buildings in the Bridge Street area, there could be rooms at less than a tenth of the cost for about 350 Members and 380 secretaries, in addition to 250 rooms within the Palace, or more if the House favoured further in-filling. It was up to the House to decide what it wanted. 'What my right hon. Friend and I want to do,' concluded Mr Channon, 'is to listen to this debate. . . . In the end, the House must decide whether to spend this £30 million to go ahead with the new parliamentary building or to adopt the cheaper solutions.'

The take-it-or-leave-it attitude of the government spokesman was very disappointing to many Members. Mr Dick Leonard, the Labour Member for Romford, castigated the Minister's speech and the government's scandalous delay in reaching a decision. 'Since 1960 the present proliferation of ugly, impracticable and scruffy buildings has continued to disfigure the area, and each year they look more forlorn and more inappropriate to their surroundings,' he declared. Proposals for the Whitehall precinct had a habit of fading away under a cloud of procrastination, infighting, inquiries and general aimlessness, and it was time to act decisively as soon as possible. The impression that this was an utterly extravagant project, an exercise in self-indulgence by sybaritic, lotus-eating Members of Parliament that was being pursued for their own convenience was quite erroneous. At present, Members had the worst facilities in Europe, he argued, but it was not the Members who would suffer. 'It is our constituents, those whom we are sent here to represent. We cannot meet them in proper conditions when they come to the House. We cannot give them the service which we ought to give them and which they rightly demand. If we value our system of parliamentary democracy, which is the true glory of this country, if we feel that the job of Member of Parliament is worth doing, and if we have any self-respect, we should equip ourselves to do the job properly.' The hon. Member concluded that the provision of this new parliamentary building was a necessary condition for doing their work. 'We shall be letting down ourselves and letting down the nation if we do not make provision for its construction in the shortest possible time.'

Sir Hugh Casson once commented that everything looks nice in a model. The Ministry had innocently sought to demonstrate the effect of the new building with several attractive and colourful drawings. In one illustration, the artist showed a young lady in conversation with Members, with her back to the viewer, wearing the then fashionable 'hot pants'. It did nothing to emphasize the seriousness of the project which Members were considering so earnestly, and had the effect on many of repelling rather than attracting their admiration. It was, they felt, like putting a girl on the bonnet of a car in the motor show, and quite inappropriate for exhibition in the House of Commons. The publicity for the building should have emphasized its grimness, not its gaiety.

For those who knew the site, there were other more practical objections. An easterly wind coming off the river tended to blow cruel clouds of dust around the corner of the Embankment, and a design which raised the building on stilts above ground level would draw the icy draughts of a winter's day into a wind tunnel. To allow the public to walk under the building and look upwards at Members on the floors above would also be an invitation to anarchists, demonstrators, terrorists and exhibitionists of every kind.

A further handicap to progress was the already notorious misjudgement on the underground car park. If there could be a mistake in calculation on that scale, by which a simple proposal for a modest amenity in the Services Committee resulted in a ten-fold increase in cost for a dubious benefit, there was every reason to suppose that inflation would raise the figure to a monstrous amount, which popular opinion would never willingly underwrite.

The original argument had been to provide facilities for Members to do their work. There was growing support for an entirely contrary view. The whole character of Parliament, complained Mr Robert Cooke, was subtly being changed by what had already been done to make Members' lives easier. 'There is no doubt,' he said, 'that by providing a lot of rooms where Members can hide themselves away, something has been lost of the quality of parliamentary life.' Although Mr Leonard had talked about having a place to meet his constituents and to work with his secretary, much of his service to his constituents lay in influencing other Members to take up the point of view of those constituents. Only by getting together a group of Members could anything be achieved.

The Member for Maidstone, Mr John Wells, pleaded for more intermingling, not for isolation 'with some secretary bird in some cubicle at the back of beyond'. Members who sat in one of the lobbies or publicly in the Library, writing their letters and gossiping with those who passed by were often doing the best work. 'That is what this place is all about,' he reiterated, 'gossiping with those who pass.' He deplored the possibility of a future in which Members, disappearing to a building outside, would then resort to push-button voting. 'The greatest jewel that this Parliament has,' he declared, 'is the certain knowledge that on Monday night the entire government will be in this Lobby or that Lobby and that I can speak if I wish to the Prime Minister of England and tell him precisely what my constituents think of him. I can see any and every one of my colleagues, and if I wish to see the Leader of the Opposition I can nobble him outside the Lobby; he will be there.'

The eloquence of the speeches for and against the new building was remarkable. The debate ran on the whole day, with the Minister announcing once more that the government would do what the House of Commons wanted. 'I must make it perfectly clear,' he said, 'that this is a matter for the House of Commons to settle, not for the government.'

Some Members wanted to decide the matter then and there; others preferred to await a further statement from the government in the light of the arguments raised for and against, and to have another debate before the final decision. By the mysterious process known as 'talking out' the debate, the desire of those who wished to vote immediately was frustrated by a Member remaining on his feet in full flow of oratory until the stroke of Big Ben reached his ears. After that, under the complicated rules of procedure, it was too late to have a division on the question and the debate was adjourned.

All the argument and the uncertainty of outcome remained deferred to an indefinite future, in spite of the plea that every month of delay was adding £115 000 to the final cost of the work.

On 25 June 1973, yet another Leader of the House (Mr James Prior) took up a brief for the new building. First he invited the House to decide whether approval should be given to a new parlimentary building. The voting on that general proposition was 292 in favour and 69 against. Then he asked the House to say whether the design by Robin Spence and Robin Webster should be chosen, and the House approved this motion by 208 votes to 144. No dates were given; in each case the decision was to be acted upon 'in due course'. It was a free vote after a short debate of only three hours, in which Mr Robert Mellish, then Opposition Chief Whip, made the shortest speech when he said, 'Whatever building is put up, there will be objections.' The heart had previously been taken out of the debate by the Chancellor of the Exchequer, who had ruled in May that no public expenditure could be incurred during the current or succeeding financial year. That statement had set back the work, if it was to be undertaken at all, until the financial year 1975–6.

The Leader of the House was cautiously in favour of the new building. 'It would not,' he thought, 'be appropriate for the Government to express a collective view other than their willingness to be guided by the decision of the House.' Everyone, said Mr Prior, must make up his mind about the look of the proposed building. Expert opinion had been sharply divided, from *The Times* which described it as a superb building to the *Daily Telegraph* which described it as little short of calamitous. Mr Prior modestly admitted that he himself was no judge of architecture and would not enter into an argument on the merits of the building, but he felt that the winning design met the needs of the House and he personally favoured it. The latest cost, with all associated works, would now be £33 million to accommodate 450 Members in single rooms, 450 secretaries and about 300 supporting staff of the House. It was tacitly assumed, though never openly declared, that this would provide a room, or a shared room, for every Member, either in the Palace itself or in the annex.

Mr Charles Pannell, who recalled that as Minister of Works he had set up the competition, pleaded for approval to be expressed in a firm decision by the House. 'It would be a devastating blow against the encouragement of young architects and the need to improve modern architecture if we lightly turn aside from all this work which has gone on at such expense and over such a long period,' he said. 'The matter started eight years ago, and after a great deal of work and disappointment, we have the result of the competition.' If it was not now approved, there could be another long-drawn-out process taking another eight years. 'We should never all agree on a building even if there were another competition. . . .' With inflation and general escalation of costs, in eight years' time the cost of a new building would be astronomical. 'Whatever the newspapers may say,' he continued, 'throughout history, as far back as the time of Samuel Pepys, most of the great writers have viewed this place with derision. It may be said that the population view it with a degree of affectionate contempt. But whenever a real crisis occurs, people say "Recall Parliament."'

As the leading advocate for the new building, Mr Charles Pannell's oratory did much to win the substantial majority by which the decision was made. He had reason to be content. With the prize-winning design approved by the Commons, all would be realized. The two young architects, already a year older, were encouraged to go ahead with practical planning and adjustment of details on the lines already laid down by the Services Committee. The Commons was at last determined to put its House in order. If the hour had not yet struck, it was surely going to, in the cautious ministerial phrase, 'in due course'.

Viewed from the south of the river, it was a disastrous decision. In April 1972, in October 1972 and in January 1973 the Greater London Council had made repeated and strong representations to the government and to Parliament against the winning design. The Council reiterated its objection to piecemeal planning, and to putting up an isolated building too high in relation to the Palace, the dominance of which had already been diminished by the short-sighted location of government offices. 'The proposed building in its present form, even though it might fit into other surroundings, is not suitable for this important position at the heart of the parliamentary and government centre of the metropolis,' declared the Council.

The new building would look bigger than any of its neighbours, dwarfing Barry's river front, diminishing Big Ben and towering over the nearby buildings on the Victoria Embankment.

These were powerful objections which seemed to deserve a considered answer by Ministers in Parliament. There was no answer in the short debate of June 1973, when the House decided to proceed with the Robin Spence and Robin Webster new building, except from Mr Charles Pannell, who declared from the Opposition benches that he could not take his views on architecture from the Greater London Council. 'Nothing that we do tonight will be as bad as the extension of County Hall across the river – that monstrosity resembling a multi-storey car park which was an eyesore and an offence to London forever, and which disfigured the approach to the House.'

CHAPTER NINETEEN

A SMALLER
MOONBEAM

1973

The House of Commons was facing a difficult winter when it resumed its sittings after a gloomy weekend in December 1973. Oil prices imposed by the Arab producers were leading to rumours of petrol rationing, to threats of petrol prices rising to the then un-heard of level of 50 pence a gallon, and to queues and ugly scenes at garages. There was also a tiresome debate in prospect for the govern-ment, involving the landscaping of New Palace Yard.

The original attraction of the now notorious underground car park beneath the Yard had been to sweep away a huddle of cars and give the space over to trees and lawns. Now, however, members of the Services Committee were again being deafened by shouts of protest from outside, following their over-hasty acceptance of the original but not too bright idea. Did they not realize that William Rufus, the son of the Conqueror, had made a yard outside West-minster Hall, not a park or a grove of trees? The Royal Fine Art Commission, the Greater London Council and the Westminster City Council were all as aghast now as they had been when the car park proposal went through the House without their opinions being canvassed. No, they told the Committee, the Yard must remain ungrassed, as a sombre forecourt to the grey old Hall, as it had always been throughout our long history. Fearful of incurring more public criticism than they had already suffered, the Services

Committee, under the leadership of Mr James Prior, accepted the authoritative advice that the entire Yard should be paved with a uniform surface of granite setts – small paving blocks – the centre area being separated from the roadway by bollards. Tree planting would be aesthetically and historically undesirable.

The open courtyard was at one time twice as large as today, and its wide expanse was relieved only by an elaborate well-head or fountain. The Royal Fine Art Commission underlined the importance of retaining what was left of its noble scale and simplicity by keeping the bare sloping surface, set off only by the row of catalpa trees, which had fringed the Yard for the past eighty or ninety years. Water or grass would produce the effect of a suburban garden instead of a monumental foreground. The idea of a mock Tudor fountain, to replace the ancient one, was rejected by the Committee, who were keeping an open mind on the creation, in its place, of a simple pool.

Nothing could have been more reasonable than the speech with which the Under Secretary of State for the Environment asked the House to approve these proposals of the Select Committee. It was, therefore, with some surprise that listeners in the gallery heard the next speaker, Mr Douglas Houghton, exclaim: 'People will wonder whether we have taken leave of our senses, because we are debating this matter at this time. . . . I regard the proposal now before the House as a smaller moonbeam in the larger lunacy.' He deplored the earlier hasty decision, but now that the Services Committee had taken 'such sage, qualified advice on what it should do with the top of the car park', he would let the advice stand. Other Members were less resigned. 'I do not believe that the proposals do justice to what is an historic, important and very valuable site. They flow from the decision to spend £2·5 million on an underground car park to cater for 500 cars . . .,' said Mr Roger Moate, recalling the useful economic purpose which New Palace Yard had hitherto served. 'No one will call the motor car, individually or collectively, a thing of beauty,' he argued. 'Nevertheless, a crowded car park at that time, the bustle of cars, and the additional activity of cars coming in up to Division Time presented part of the modern Westminster scene. It was a useful car park. It was alive. Now, by contrast, we intend to make it a vast space and by contrast it appears sterile.'

Mr Phillip Whitehead was anxious about the reactions of his constituents when he told them how much time had been spent in the discussion on what to do in New Palace Yard. 'I must say, if I can do so and still remain within the rules of order, that this is a fatuous debate.' He had one suggestion for the Minister. It was that part of the Yard should be used for recreation. He recalled the historical fact that tennis balls dating from the reign of Henry VIII were found in the beams of Westminster Hall when the roof was being repaired, showing that royal tennis had been played there. He, therefore, suggested that two tennis courts might be put in the middle of New Palace Yard to enable Members to keep fit 'and discover that there are more things for which one's right arm can be used than in other places of recreation in this building'.

Apart from throwing out that suggestion for the government to think over, he deplored the three hours allocated for this debate. 'It seems,' the Member concluded, 'the most absurd comment on current events since Louis XVI entered "Nothing" in his diary on the day of the storming of the Bastille.'

One Member admired the fan-shaped scallops of small granite blocks already embedded in the ground, while another was concerned about their cost and would prefer to vary the surface with water and grass. There was some support for a pool which might reflect the buildings on each side of the Yard. Other Members warned that visitors tended to throw cigarette packets and waste paper into still water. There was more talk about tree planting, depth of soil, the cost of car-parking spaces, reckoned at £5000 per car, the life of the existing catalpas, the possibility of *son et lumière*, the parking of sedan chairs before the days of coaching and the fact that the fountain in New Palace Yard was decorated for the coronation of Henry IV in 1399. 'The long and short of it,' commented Mr Michael English, 'is that we are making a rather long-winded nonsense about the matter. Having said that, I shall sit down.'

The debate ranged on for a further hour. At length, the House voted on the proposals of the Services Committee and on a division negatived their plan, thereby endorsing at least on this occasion Barry's description of Commons Committees as being 'of all the tribunals the most unfit to decide'.

The unexpected rejection of the Services Committee's report by the House was a shock to the traditionalists, for the decision meant that a 'pretty' grass and fountain setting would now replace the austere yard which had its antecedents in William Rufus's time. The mechanical shovels, however, which were excavating the five underground levels of the car park, now produced a minor historical bonus. A report entitled 'Archaeological Investigations in New Palace Yard, 1972–3', gave details of the discovery of the octagonal foundation of the Great Conduit, built in the early fifteenth century, which incorporated the remains of a twelfth-century fountain. Unfortunately, these ruins could not be adapted for any decorative purpose in the car park scheme.

CHAPTER TWENTY

ARCHITECTURAL
HERITAGE

1975

The European Architectural Heritage Year of 1975 brought one incidental benefit to Westminster. Members discovered that on their own doorstep, newly cleaned, was a pink and white building designed under Dutch influence by Norman Shaw, who was born three years before the Great Fire of 1834 and lived into George V's reign. It was a lively piece of architecture, Norman Shaw's only major public building; its pink brick was capped with stone gables and crowned at each end by an obelisk. Even to the inexpert eye, it made a happy addition to the line of solemn grey structures along the river front, without in any way breaking up their harmony.

A few years earlier, the building had been due for demolition by the government after its occupiers, the Metropolitan Police, had moved out, carrying with them to a glass block on Victoria Street the name by which it had long been known – New Scotland Yard. With unusual foresight, the Services Committee had as early as March 1973 recommended the use of Norman Shaw's building for House of Commons purposes, irrespective of the decision on the proposed new building in Bridge Street. By 1975 the conversion from police use to occupation by Members was complete. The Leader of the House (now Mr Edward Short) described it as 'a splendid piece of work, which reflects great credit on those who carried it out'.

The north section, after conversion, provided rooms for 128 Members. 'When I first walked into my office, I thought I had walked into the Savoy because of the superfluous luxury of the place,' observed Mr Nicholas Fairbairn, a Scottish Tory. The subsequent conversion of the south section, when completed, would be adequate for another 80 Members.

The rediscovery of Norman Shaw's building, which was constructed in two sections, north and south, greatly reduced the demand for space within the Palace of Westminster. Members found that even without a travelator they could reach the Chamber within the six minutes allowed before the lobby doors are locked for a division. Bridge Street itself, even at the height of traffic congestion, could be crossed by using the existing subway, and Edward Barry's colonnade gave protection from the weather as Members walked along the edge of New Palace Yard. A considerable inconvenience was involved in leaving one building and going into another several minutes away, but it was not insuperable.

Two years had passed since the House had decisively voted in favour of the new building by Robin Spence and Robin Webster; after distinguished work in detailed planning over those two years they were still awaiting the government's order to proceed with construction. On 16 July 1975 the Commons was told in a statement by the Leader, Mr Edward Short, that the engagement of the architects was to be brought to an immediate end. In view of inflation, Mr Short said, it would not be right to proceed with the scheme. The estimated costs had already reached at least £30 million, excluding the site costs already incurred. Apart from the Norman Shaw building, there were others in the Bridge Street area which would provide rooms for Members, and, in the circumstances, that solution must be accepted. He thanked the two architects, who were to be fairly compensated, and expressed his personal regret 'that it should end this way'. Nobody appeared to be surprised at the news. Mr Peyton, for the Opposition, welcomed 'that rather oddly timed statement. We congratulate the government on bowing to the inevitable. We should also like to be associated with what the right hon. Gentleman said about sympathy with the architects.'

The dream, the years of controversy, the years of planning and of financial effort were all over. Symbolically, the young lime trees newly planted on top of the underground car park in New Palace Yard wilted and died. Reinforced concrete had not proved the kindliest soil.

The thirty-five years since the Germans had bombed the Victorian building had seen many opportunities lost, many failures to decide and much money wasted. A room for every Member had emerged little by little as a desirable goal, but was never firmly admitted to be a necessity. As late as July 1975 Mr Tam Dalyell was still reminding the Commons of his own unremitting campaign for more space. 'Can some tactful hints be dropped in the direction of the Lord Chancellor?' he asked the Leader of the House. 'Is it a fact that he has fifty-six rooms? Is it not also a fact that eleven years ago some of us discovered in an area of 590 square feet a man pressing his trousers? In the past decade that area of the Palace of Westminster has not been altered.'

The traditional timidity of the government of the day, irrespective of party, in dealing broadly with any matter of concern to Parliament was still noticeable. Mr Dalyell got little satisfaction from his intervention beyond the knowledge that his questions had been noted, and were recorded in *Hansard* for a future generation to reflect upon.

Meanwhile, more blocking out of windows, more squalid infilling of courtyards and more building of huts on the roofs of the nineteenth-century edifice were already being planned and have since been carried out. As each new Committee of Members was set up, more space had to be found for committee staff; more shelving for documents, more secretaries and typists, more telephones and photo-copying machines, more researchers, more filing cabinets to contain the files, more messengers to carry them and more specialists were brought into the already crowded building. In a loyal if ludicrous attempt to meet the needs of Members, the Committee clerks bisected one of their offices not only vertically but horizontally as well, with an unsteady upper floor introduced near the top of Barry's tall windows, making box-like containers out of the original room. The private residences of officials, which Edward Barry suggested in 1867 need not be so close to the House, are still within the main building encumbering the floor space to within yards of the debating chamber. Only the underground car park in New Palace Yard remains to demonstrate the capacity of Members themselves to contribute at great public expense something novel in character and style.

Inspired by the best of motives, desecration of the Palace has been both continuous and, in total, more expensive than the drastic solution of moving Parliament to another site, which a minority of Members advocated after the Second World War. One decision, however, would have delighted the original designer of the new Palace of Westminster and more than justified his hopes. The Victoria Tower, Charles Barry's finest creation, has been quietly brought to a state of perfection which would not have been possible in his time. Everything about the structure involved a problem, but its purpose was to be a store-house of parliamentary records, and above everything else it had to be a fireproof repository.

On the night of the great fire of 1834, a junior but percipient Lords official named Smith threw hundreds of bundles of Lords documents out of the blazing windows on to Old Palace Yard. Among them were a packet of letters which had been abandoned by King Charles I at the battle of Naseby, the original Book of Common Prayer of 1662, the Declaration of Breda and many rare manuscripts. The historical importance of such public papers won slow recognition after 1870 in the reports from the newly formed Royal Commission on Historical Manuscripts, and papers of value were put into the strong rooms of the Victoria Tower and then forgotten. The Second World War brought one or two side benefits which were scarcely recognized at the time.

The Commons set up a Select Committee on the Disposal and Custody of Documents, more with the intention of re-cycling waste paper than of retaining precious manuscripts. Its chairman, Sir Dennis Herbert, listened with patient gravity to a monocled officer from the Ministry of Supply who proposed to him in secrecy an idea for adapting parchment from Bills and Public Petitions for the manufacture of soldiers' boots. That proposition did not find acceptance, but as a result of this Committee some of the more valuable Commons documents began to be regularly transferred for storage to the House of Lords and deposited in the Victoria Tower.

After the war, so the story goes, a Ministry official was concerned with the installation of a boiler which involved digging the soft clay under one of the courtyards. Looking up, he could have sworn he saw the Tower above him beginning to lean. The accidental benefit of a threatened collapse of the whole structure enabled the Ministry of Works to undertake a costly but brilliant piece of internal engineering, designed to replace or reinforce the cast-iron pillars of Barry's day on which nine floors above the Royal Entrance depended.

It had always been beyond the agility of Select Committees to chase 553 steps up the Tower to quiz the architects on what was to happen at the top. The problem could be considered without interference from Members of either House. A contemporary journal explained the slowness with which Sir Charles Barry had proceeded on the highest stone-built tower in England. It was 'in order to give the weary earth time to concentrate its powers of endurance beneath such a Cyclopean structure'. An appreciation of the problems which he had tried with only partial success to overcome now emerged from the Ministry's new architectural study.

Above the great vault of the Royal Entrance was a small sliding trap door. When it was opened, the roof floor of the Tower, hundreds of feet higher, could be seen from the carriageway far below. Rising from the flagstones of the well floor above the Royal Entrance, the two Barrys had built a spiral cast-iron staircase, described by a modern architect (Mr J. W. Worricker) as 'a masterpiece of Victorian ingenuity. . . . An example of one of the earliest and most remarkable instances of the cast-iron stair worker's art ever to be built in this country.' The whole way up this stairway ran a mahogany handrail almost without a visible join.

The staircase itself must have been constructed on site, with molten lead giving further security to the bolts which held it together as a single unit, rigid and immovable. On the landings were heavy iron doors, each set with a judas window, leading to the strong rooms in which the records of Parliament were to be stored. Ominously, however, as the climber ascended towards the top of the Tower many locked doors were marked 'No Access'. Floors had never been built in some of the upper strong rooms of which the doors were supposed to be entrances. It is assumed that the floors were omitted because the dangers of overloading must have become apparent to the original architects, particularly after Edward Barry had completed the roof, with its ornately carved balustrade and seventy-two-foot flagstaff, after his father's death.

The outward purpose of the Tower was purely ornamental; inside it was to provide a magnificent repository 'wherein are to be preserved the muniments of the legislature of the nation'. How poorly this aim had at first been carried out had been shown in the well justified complaints of Sir Herbert Williams in 1944. Dank and mildewed documents of immense historical value lay heaped on the stone floors; pigeons and even a kestrel flew in and out of broken windows. A solitary old and underpaid retainer was in charge, making an occasional despairing climb, when the weather was warm enough, up the spiral stairs, and keeping a totally inaccurate list of the Tower's contents in a small notebook. Before the Ministry's rescue operation began, the interior of the Tower was described as 'exceedingly damp and unbelievably filthy'.

To remedy the peril of an overstressed tower is an operation involving immense skill and a great deal of luck. First, the top four floors, which had never been used, were lightened by the removal of 450 tons of material. Regretfully the architects had to take out all but the first eighty feet of the splendid staircase. A set of sixteen 20-ton jacks were set in position to transfer the remaining roof load of 276 tons on to new steel girders, which had to be welded into place after their introduction into the Tower. On the day appointed for the hazardous lifting, special gauges were set to register any movement of the structure, all but a few experts left the building and whistles were to be blown to warn the operators of the lifting gear of danger. There were tense moments when on 15 October 1959 the lifting operation began, but it was successfully accomplished in a day with the alarm only being sounded once.

Saving the Tower from collapse was only half the task. The next step was to turn it into a modern muniment store. The problem of access was dealt with by replacing the old cell-like rooms with a single large chamber on each of seven upper floors, served by one of the longest running lifts in the country. Light painted walls and orange floor covering, constantly maintained by a full-time cleaning staff, avoided the previous build-up of dust and dirt.

Five and a half miles of metal racking was installed to house three million documents. Among the thousands of parchment rolls is an Act a third of a mile long, a manuscript record of the trial of Mary, Queen of Scots, the Act of Habeas Corpus, the original Bill of Rights, the Reform Act of 1832 and vast numbers of local petitions.

New ventilation, infinitely superior to anything elsewhere in the Palace, would have delighted the heart of Dr David Boswell Reid. No smoking is allowed, an absolute prohibition since the slightest trace of smoke sucked through the air extracter ducts will set the fire alarm system ringing throughout the Tower. Incoming air, before reaching the strong rooms where books and records are stored, passes through resin wool microbiological filters and through alkali beds which absorb acidic moisture. As a result of the careful monitoring of humidity and temperature, even the oldest documents are now clear of mould spores, either active or latent. Lighting is by fluorescent tubes fitted with white plastic shields to prevent eye-strain on the part of the Record Office staff, who work in conditions that Members might well envy.

The appointment of an exceptionally gifted Clerk of the Records, Mr Maurice Bond, facilitated the transformation of the repository from its former dismal state to one of the historical showpieces of Britain. The staff of the new Record Office make the contents of the Tower available to the public throughout the year. A telephone call in advance of the visit is all that is required for an item to be produced from the nation's records of possibly five centuries ago, endorsed in Norman French. The sounds of modern London grow faint as the researcher takes his place near a window overlooking Edward the Confessor's Old Palace Yard and the Abbey. The atmosphere is one of monastic peace, recalling Westminster's precious past which was so nearly lost by neglect.

On the staircase of the Lower Waiting Hall down in the Commons, Charles Barry, the architect who never achieved full recognition, is portrayed leaning over his drawing board, pencil in hand. The sculptor, Foley, has outlined in firm strokes on the drawing board Barry's final work, the Victoria Tower. Its interior was beyond his powers to complete, but its original purpose has at last been splendidly realized.

INDEX

INDEX